D1570153

LOOK AT THE
SUNLIGHT
ON THE WATER

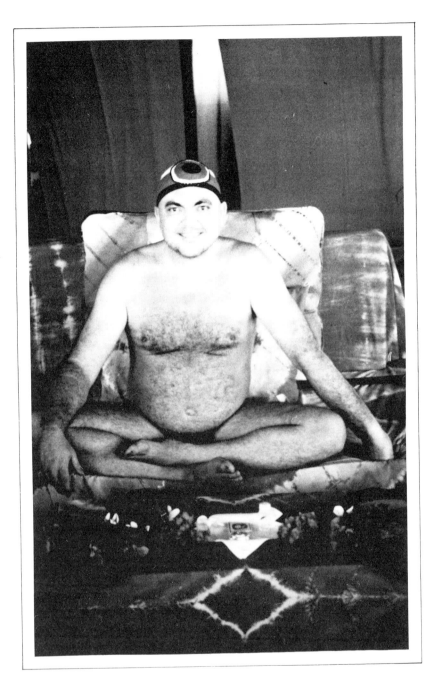

LOOK AT THE SUNLIGHT ON THE WATER

Educating Children for a Life of
Self-Transcending Love and Happiness

HEART-MASTER DA

(The Avadhoota Da Love-Ananda Hridayam,
Whose Teaching Name Is Da Free John)

THE DAWN HORSE PRESS
SAN RAFAEL, CALIFORNIA

First edition September 1983
Reprinted in July 1984, November 1987
Printed in the United States of America
International Standard Book Number: paper 0-913922-84-6
Library of Congress Catalog Card Number: 83-72847

Produced by The Free Daist Communion in cooperation with The Dawn Horse Press

CONTENTS

NOTE TO THE READER

All material in this book for which authorship is not clearly stated has been contributed by the editors. This includes the introductions to parts 1, 2, and 3 and Tables 1–4 at the end of part 2.

"I Am No Other"

The Sacrificial Life and Blessing Work of Heart-Master Da

F rom the moment of His birth, on November 3, 1939, in Jamaica, Long Island, New York, Heart-Master Da has been moved to bring others into His own Enlightened Condition. And this Compassionate Motive to Awaken others has required a series of almost inconceivable Sacrifices on His part. Born Illumined, He spent His earliest years consciously alive as "a radiant form, a source of energy, bliss and light".[1]—a Condition that He later called the "Bright".[2] But even during those early childhood days, He was troubled by the un-Happiness of those around Him, who seemed unaware of His direct communication of His (and their own) Condition.

The great Love that from the start has been His outstanding characteristic moved Him spontaneously to forgo His Unconditionally Happy and Free State and to assume the state of those around Him, who were suffering in dilemma. His Impulse was to discover a way to communicate to others the Freedom and Humor of His "Bright" Radiance and Unbounded Consciousness. For it was clear to Him that all Are as He Is, except that they are

---

1. Heart-Master Da, *The Knee of Listening: The Early Life and Radical Spiritual Teachings of Heart-Master Da (Da Free John)* (San Rafael, Calif.: The Dawn Horse Press, 1984), p. 9.

2. The "Bright" is the term Heart-Master Da used as a child to describe the Self-Radiant Love-Bliss that was His Condition at birth. It is the Self-Radiant Condition of Transcendental Divine Existence. It is His own Ultimate Realization, and it is the Realization of all devotees who enter the seventh or Divinely Enlightened stage of life.

The "Bright" (and its variations, such as "Brightness" and the adjective "Bright") is also Heart-Master Da's technical term for Self-Radiant Consciousness Itself, which includes and yet transcends all conditional forms and events, even the entire cosmos. In itself, the "Bright" is the Eternal Realm of unqualified and uncreated Conscious Light, the "Divine Self-Domain", which Heart-Master Da has said is neither "here" nor "there" but which transcends space-time in the Divine Itself, "Where You Stand", prior to conditional existence. And in the context of conditional existence, the "Bright" is Realized as the Self-Illuminated (literally Enlightened) Structure of all worlds and forms.

i

unaware of the Divine Happiness that is their Native Condition. This spontaneous relinquishment of the "Bright" was His first great Sacrifice, undertaken at a little more than two years old. Thus, the stage was set for the first major cycle in the Divine Ordeal that is the life of Heart-Master Da.

Throughout Heart-Master Da's childhood the "Bright" progressively receded from consciousness. It resurfaced only occasionally in breakthroughs of "Cosmic Consciousness" or "Savikalpa Samadhi"[3] that molded His Spiritual development and reinforced His Heroic Impulse to discover the Way of God-Realization for modern men and women. And finally, when the "Bright" had receded to the point that He could no longer contact It as a Source of Happiness, Heart-Master Da began His Ordeal of Realization. Through thirteen years of the most intensive struggle—with self, with the doubting mood of Western civilization, and with the universal taboo against Ecstatic Identification with the Supreme Being—He undertook a Spiritual journey that was to lead Him over the face of three continents and through countless trials. He threw Himself into the drama of His Spiritual unfolding without any holding back, often pushing Himself to the point of sheer despair.

3. The Sanskrit term "Savikalpa Samadhi" means literally "concentration, or absorption, with form". It is the experience of ecstasy associated with subtle perception beyond the experiential context of the physical body. Heart-Master Da has indicated that there are two varieties of "Savikalpa Samadhi". The first is the experience of subtle forms, which may occur in meditation or even arise spontaneously in extraordinary states of psycho-physical awareness. The second is what Heart-Master Da calls "Cosmic Consciousness", or the Vision of Cosmic Unity, which is the highest form of Savikalpa Samadhi.

When Cosmic Consciousness is experienced as an isolated or periodic occurrence, attention ascends spontaneously to a state of awareness wherein conditional existence is perceived as a unity in Divine Consciousness. Since this "conditional" form of Cosmic Consciousness, which is pursued in the paths of Yogic and mystical ascent, depends upon the manipulation of the body-mind, and is interpreted from the point of view of the separate self, it should thus be differentiated from Enlightenment, or God-Realization, in which the psycho-physical world (including the body-mind) is perceived from the "Point of View" of the Spiritual and Transcendental Divine Self rather than the body-mind. This Condition, which Heart-Master Da calls "Sahaj Samadhi" and also "Open Eyes", and which may also be seen as a kind of "unconditional" Cosmic Consciousness, is the "perception" or Realization of all phenomenal states as merely apparent modifications of the inherent Self-Radiance of the Transcendental Divine Self.

Sahaj Samadhi was Heart-Master Da's constant Enjoyment in infancy and early childhood. And even after He had relinquished the "Bright" of His childhood, Cosmic Consciousness, viewed conditionally from the point of view of the body-mind, continued to break through in His life periodically and spontaneously, until the event of His Radical Re-Awakening.

His odyssey began in 1957 when, at the age of seventeen, He entered Columbia College. There, through the intensity of His search, He quickly reached the dead end of possibilities for self-fulfillment through mental knowledge and bodily experiences and underwent a temporary breakthrough experience of the cosmic consciousness of His childhood. The Ordeal continued in northern California (during and after graduate work at Stanford University in 1961), where He began to explore the vast realm of psychic potential. In the mid-1960s Heart-Master Da extended His adventure into conscious exploration of traditional esoteric Yoga and mysticism, and He fulfilled all the traditional Realizations a human being may enjoy prior to God-Realization, ultimately transcending them all in Enlightenment Itself. He conducted His practice principally in the eastern United States and in India, receiving the aid and initiatory Blessings of Spiritual Teachers both in the flesh and in subtle form. Finally, He was led by a Divine Vision on a pilgrimage from India through Europe and ultimately to Los Angeles. There in a small temple of the Vedanta Society in Hollywood, on September 10, 1970, Heart-Master Da Awoke permanently to the Spiritual and Transcendental Divine Self, or Consciousness Itself.

This Awakening began the second cycle of the Love-Sacrifice that is His life. His was an even greater destiny than to struggle beyond the limitations of an ordinary life and Realize the Self-Existing and Self-Radiant Consciousness that is the native (if latent) Condition of every man and woman. Now He began the more difficult struggle of communicating that Realization to others. After the Event in the Vedanta Temple, whenever He sat in meditation, countless others appeared to Him, and, assuming no separation from them, He did their meditation in the form of His own body-mind. When many of these individuals began to appear in life face to face with Him, He took up the arduous Teaching Ordeal for which His Realization had prepared Him.

For more than seventeen years, He engaged those who came to Him in all kinds of instructive occasions, laboring Compasssionately to show them the Way of Realization whereby they might understand their suffering as their own activity and go beyond it. At first, He simply Taught the "Radical"[4] Truth of Consciousness that had become obvious in His Realization. But those who came to Him were unable to respond to this pure Offering of Truth. Their problems in life occupied nearly all of their interest, so that very little energy and attention were left over for the Radical Process of Awakening. And that minimal response was not nearly sufficient to allow His Work to be effective.

Consequently, just as He had Sacrificed His enjoyment of the "Bright" in childhood, He now abandoned Himself to His sacrificial relationship with the people who had come to Him. Without losing sight of the Radical Truth that had become simply Obvious to Him under all conditions, He entered into the lives of those people, Working with them in the thick of the problems that bound them. When He had first begun to Teach, He was still known by His given name, "Franklin Albert Jones". In 1973, He spontaneously assumed the Name "Bubba Free John". This use of His childhood nickname "Bubba" signalled His willingness to live in brotherly familiarity with people until they could acknowledge His "Bright" Condition and relate to Him formally as Guru, or True Heart-Master. He lived among them as a Spiritual Friend, examining and exploring with them—always to the point of clarity and equanimity—every area of life in which they were bound.

His was no ordinary "friendship". Because He Worked so directly with those who came to Him, many people found their attention consistently attracted to Him, and, through His Agency, to the Divine Revelation. In His Compassion for those who came to Him, He provided a steady stream of Spiritual Instruction, constantly realigning people to right practice and to reception of His Transmission of Mere and Blessing Presence. By means of His "Siddhi" (or Spiritual and Transcendental Divine Transmission) of the Heart[5], during the years of His Teaching Work people found themselves capable of a degree of

4. While the popular usage of "radical" indicates an extreme (usually political) position or view, Heart-Master Da uses the term "Radical" in its original and primary sense, deriving from the Latin "radix", meaning "root", and by extension meaning "irreducible", "fundamental", or "relating to the origin". In contrast to the progressive or evolutionary paths of the world's exoteric and esoteric religious and Spiritual traditions, the "Radical" or irreducible Process directly and immediately penetrates or transcends the ego at its fundamental root or origin, the self-contraction at the heart.

5. The "Heart" is another name for the Divine Self, the Intuition or Realization of Self-Existing and Self-Radiant Transcendental Divine Being (or God). The origin of the term is the experiential association of Transcendental Self-Realization with the sense of the release of

self-understanding and Spiritual practice that would otherwise have been impossible. By temporarily Awakening, through His Teaching Siddhis, the signs of advanced practice in those whose qualifications were otherwise ordinary, He developed and elaborated the necessary lessons and essential instructions for every stage of the Way of the Heart, and Demonstrated for all, the essential practice and the unique Potency of relationship between the True Heart-Master and His devotee.

Even in the earliest years of His Teaching Work, Heart-Master Da unfailingly turned those who came to Him toward the primacy of Satsang,[6] or God-Communion via the Spiritual relationship to the True Heart-Master and the Divine Person, which is the essential Principle of the Way of the Heart. He Instructed them extensively in practice of the Way of Satsang, or what He later came to call "Ishta-Guru-Bhakti Yoga"—the Yoga of devotion ("Bhakti") to the Living Divine Person through Communion with the True Heart-Master (the "Ishta-Guru", or the Beloved "chosen" by the heart). Ishta-Guru-Bhakti Yoga, which is founded on the self-understanding that awakens by granting attention to the True Heart-Master's recorded Teaching-Revelation, is the practice of moment to moment Communion with and Realization of the Divine Condition made obvious in the "Mere and Blessing Presence"[7] of the True Heart-Master. The practice of Ishta-Guru-Bhakti Yoga is the central Revelation of Heart-Master Da's Teaching

---

identification with the separate self sense felt in the right side of the chest, and the sense of the falling (or dissolution) of the mind (or process of thought and attention) into its Root or Origin in the "Locus" associated with the trunk of the body.

"Siddhi" is a Sanskrit term meaning "power" or "accomplishment". When capitalized, in Heart-Master Da's Teaching Word, it refers to the "Power of the Heart", or the spontaneous and Perfect Consciousness, Presence, and Power of the very Divine, Which is Transmitted to living beings through the unobstructed Agency of the True Heart-Master or "Siddha", one whose Enlightenment is perfect and who is Graced with the spontaneous Capacity to Awaken others.

The uncapitalized term (siddhi) refers to various Yogic processes and psychic abilities. The lesser siddhis may be either sought or shunned in most traditional paths. In the Way of the Heart, they may arise spontaneously, in which case they are allowed, observed, and understood.

6. "Satsang" literally means "true or right relationship", "the company of Truth". It is commonly or traditionally used to refer to the practice of spending time in the company of holy or wise persons. One can also enjoy Satsang with a holy place, a venerated image, the burial shrine of a saint, or with the Spiritual and Transcendental Divine Person. Heart-Master Da uses the term in its fullest sense to signify the very relationship between the True Heart-Master (and, by His Agency, the Divine Person) and His devotee. That relationship is seen to be an all-inclusive Condition, effective at every level of life and consciousness.

7. Even from the beginning of His Teaching Work Heart-Master Da has spoken of His "Mere and Blessing Presence" as the most effective means of Grace. The Mere and Blessing Presence of

Work, as it is also the ancient essence of religion and esoteric Spirituality.

During His more than seventeen years of Teaching Work, Heart-Master Da Gifted practitioners of the Way of the Heart in countless ways. In fact, the Sacred Name or Title of God-Realization "Da", which He Revealed in 1979, is honored in many sacred traditions as a primal Word-Sound that means "the Divine Giver of Life and Liberation". Foremost among the Sacred Offerings of Heart-Master Da are the Agencies and Instruments of Blessing Transmission that He has established. The more than thirty volumes of His magnificent Wisdom-Teaching, which document the Work He did as Teacher, clarify and elaborate all aspects of the Way of the Heart. And He has Blessed and Empowered three Meditation Sanctuaries (The Mountain of Attention in northern California, Tumomama in Hawaii, and Translation Island Hermitage in Fiji).

Always in the course of His Teaching Work Heart-Master Da reminded practitioners of the Radical Truth that, once most fundamentally understood, awakens the capacity to penetrate all problems and dilemmas and transcend phenomenal existence absolutely. During those seventeen years, He continually Graced practitioners with the Divine Radiance and Spirit-Energy, penetrating Insight, profound Wisdom, and unquenchable Happiness that are the abundant Offering of His Unconditional Love. Yet His magnificent Teaching Work had only a limited effect in terms of permanently Awakening practitioners to the Liberating Truth that is Heart-Master Da's real and Radical Message. People did become happier and more responsible in their lives, and the love relationship between the True Heart-Master and those who came to Him grew deep and strong and abiding. But still they persisted in the habits of un-Enlightenment. They held to their problematic and self-concerned refusal of His ultimate Gift: the Radical Realization of Consciousness Itself and inherent Happiness.

---

the True Heart-Master communicates His universal Heart-Baptism, or His Blessing Transmission of Awakening Power (whereby the Divine Condition is directly Realized). This Mere and Blessing Presence is magnified for (or linked to) human beings by the Work of the True Heart-Master's human Incarnation. However, His Mere and Blessing Presence is Self-Radiant and Self-Existing, prior to limitations of space and time, body and mind. Therefore, once He establishes Fully Empowered Agencies and Instruments, the Transmission of His Mere and Blessing Presence no longer depends on His physical Company, or even His physical embodiment.

As He continually pointed out, their failure to Realize the Truth was simply a refusal. It can be called nothing else, since they had been given all necessary Instruction and Help time after time, and always in fresh, clear, incisive lessons that cut through every problem and at last—as they themselves often acknowledged to Him—temporarily Revealed the Divine Condition and Reality.

The stubborn refusal of humanity to bow to Truth is almost universally underestimated, even though the sacred traditions are filled with examples of rejection of the True Heart-Master's Gift of Blessing and even betrayal of the True Heart-Master Himself. Only the True Heart-Master feels the full burden of the struggle that is the Spiritual Process, for Heart-Master Da's life is spent to ease the Way of Realization for all. Yet even with His great Help, to live the Way of the True Heart requires everything of a man or woman. Inevitably, the ancient drama of rejection unfolds in each person's case as the ego-bound individual, reaching the limit of his or her ability to engage the process of self-transcendence, hardens his or her heart to the Adept's Call. This is the most difficult test for every practitioner, and to pass beyond it requires a conversion to love that is uncommon in human history.

The True Heart-Master's Work with people undergoing the difficulties of that conversion exacts a high price. In His Realization, He enjoys Divine Freedom and Love-Bliss. But in His human embrace of those still struggling against His Call for self-transcendence, He is utterly vulnerable, without defenses against the destructive self-possession of those He has dedicated His life to serve, and He suffers their continual acts of rejection and unlove as a deep and never-healing wound.

This refusal of people to receive His Gift of Realization brought the Great Lover Heart-Master Da to the crisis that initiated His third Heroic cycle of Sacrifice. He came to feel that His Teaching Work was doomed to fail because of their unconscious, stubborn, ego-bound refusal to receive His Supreme Gift of Realization. After all His labors, Heart-Master Da despaired of His only Purpose for being alive—to fully Awaken great numbers of devotees. And in the moment of utmost despair, He gave up His Teaching Work and died.

In that actual, physical death, which occurred on Translation Island, the Hermitage Sanctuary in Fiji, on January 11, 1986, the truly Radical stage of His Work was born. As His personal physician and a few of His closest intimates gathered around His still and lifeless form, He re-entered the body once more. He did not come back to re-engage His active Teaching Work, for He had seen the failure of it, and, though the process of bringing His Teaching Work to a close would yet require many months of effort, His relinquishment of it was final. Nor did He come back simply to Radiate Divine Blessing to the humanity He had been born to serve, for He saw no way that human beings could truly receive what He had to Offer. Instead, He returned to life only out of Love, free at last of His Teaching Purpose, and only Full of Heart-Attraction to those He had come to Love in the most deeply human manner.

Paradoxically, only in the relinquishment of His Teaching struggle was the means for the fulfillment of the Way of the Heart finally established. In this Great Event Heart-Master Da incarnated His Divine Realization and Love more fully than ever before, as, drawn by His Love for all humanity, He took on the human condition without reservation. In His effortless, complete, Loving Embrace of humanity, His Divine Agency was magnified beyond compare.

Heart-Master Da's Death in Hermitage was only the beginning of the profound and spontaneous process of "Divine Indifference",[8] or demonstrated Freedom from all concern for arising conditions. Such Divinely Enlightened Indifference is not signed by artificial vows or the ascetic exclusion of any dimension of life, although His Divine Indifference is Revealed, in part, by Heart-Master Da's "Power of

---

8. Heart-Master Da has described the process of inherently Spiritual and Transcendental Divine Self-Realization, or the Ultimate Yoga of the Enlightened individual, as a demonstration that takes place in four stages—"Divine Transfiguration", "Divine Transformation", "Divine Indifference", and "Outshining" or "Divine Translation".

"Divine Indifference" is inherent Freedom expressed as a lack of "concern" relative to all conditional objects, relations, and states. In the Way of the Heart, "Divine Indifference" stands in contrast to the ascetical, or life-negative, viewpoint, which colors much of traditional religion and Spirituality, and which is epitomized by the strategic exclusion of conditional appearances. Rather than seeking to cling to the Transcendental Position by excluding conditional existence, the "Divine Indifference" of Enlightenment does not attempt to avoid or escape any conditions. It is characterized by Freedom in relation to conditional appearances and "A Motiveless (or Non-Strategic) Disposition Of Mere Self-Radiance (or "Bright" Self-Absorption In The Perfectly Subjective Source Of Cosmic Existence)" (*The Dawn Horse Testament*). "Divine Indifference" is discussed fully in chapter 44 of *The Dawn Horse Testament*.

Renunciation", or the ability to perform penance in His own body-mind for the sake of all beings. But the primary sign of Divine Indifference is in Heart-Master Da's ongoing relinquishment of the need to Teach those bound by the motives and programs of conventional existence.

At this turning point in His Work, Heart-Master Da adopted new Names and Titles, chief among them being the Name "Love-Ananda" and the Title (or Designation) "Hridayam". The Name "Love-Ananda", meaning "the Divine Love-Bliss", was spontaneously given to Him in 1969 by Swami Muktananda,[9] His principal Spirit-Baptizer during the course of His Spiritual practice. And the Designation "Hridayam", meaning the "True (or Spiritual, Transcendental, and Divine) Heart", signals the Divine Compassion with which He takes His Place at the heart of every being, Standing eternally for all as the Guide to the "Divine Self-Domain".[10] He Is the Heart, the Self-Existing and Self-Radiant Source of Life and Consciousness, the One Being Who Liberates all beings from suffering and bewilderment. Just as the Vedanta Temple Event signalled the end of "Franklin Jones" (the Spiritual seeker) and the beginning of the Teaching Work, the Death in Hermitage was a Sign of the approaching Retirement of the Spiritual Teacher "Da Free John" and the unfolding of the Blessing Work of the Heart-Master "Da Love-Ananda".

Heart-Master Da appears at a critical moment in human history, when humanity stands either on the brink of global catastrophe, even nuclear holocaust, or on the road to worldwide cooperation and a rebirth of Spiritual values. The ancient esoteric Wisdom from sacred traditions of all times and cultures, though shrouded in archaisms and cultural idiosyncrasies, is openly published for all to study. Yet people remain without real self-understanding, bound to the lowest spectrum of human possibilities, and the Truth and the True Heart-Master are universally doubted and made the subject of ridicule. Freely assuming

9. Swami Muktananda Paramahansa was born May 16, 1908, in Mangalore, South India, and died on October 2, 1982. An Indian Adept of Kundalini Yoga, Swami Muktananda served Heart-Master Da as Spiritual Teacher during the period from 1968 to 1970.

10. Heart-Master Da ecstatically affirms that there is a Divine Self-Domain, which is the "Bright" Destiny of the God-Realized devotee and which transcends space-time and is thus beyond the mind's capacity to comprehend or describe. That Domain is not other than the Heart Itself. Realization of the Divine Self-Domain as the Spiritual and Transcendental Divine Self or Consciousness is the principal subject of Heart-Master Da's Wisdom-Teaching.

the most difficult imaginable task, Avadhoota Da Love-Ananda Hridayam—armed with the Power of the Heart—comes at this pivotal juncture with the expressed intent to make a difference in the scale of history. Already He has produced a Teaching literature that is unprecedented in its scope and Wisdom, stating freshly the ancient Truth that alone can awaken modern minds from their sulk of doubt. But He has come to do more than Teach. He has come to Offer the direct Realization of that Truth to all who will receive His Gift.

And at the close of His Teaching Work, Heart-Master Da once again reconsidered with students and practitioners all the necessary lessons and instructions of the Way of the Heart, closing any "loopholes" in understanding that might permit people to mis-interpret the profundity of His Call and thereby to dilute the demand of practice or to bypass the necessarily self-transcending Ordeal of the Spiritual Process. He brought practitioners to more fully understand and appreciate the integrity and profundity of the practice of listening and pondering that leads to hearing, or most fundamental self-understanding. And He re-emphasized the necessity, when hearing has awakened, to actively embrace most fundamental self-under-standing as a self-transcending discipline, applying this Radical Under-standing in every area of life. Through His Instruction, students and practitioners became firmly grounded in the listening-hearing process that prepares the heart for the Radical, or direct, Realization of the Divine Person and Condition. And by these means the foundations were laid for people to truly begin to practice as devotees, thereby allowing Him to bring His Teaching Work to an end.

Now, finished with the need to Work in the Teaching mode, Heart-Master Da simply Stands Free (Where He Is and As He Is), Boundlessly Radiant in all directions, always and only Merely Present. From His "Blessing-Seat" (wherever He resides), He is always magnifying the Siddhi of the Heart to all. Therefore, even if few have personal contact with Him in His human Form, He will always continue to do His Blessing Work, planting in the hearts of devotees (when they appear) and potential devotees throughout the world the seeds of the Realization of Consciousness and Love-Bliss as the always present Condition of every one. Through responsive reception of Heart-Master Da's Spiritually Transmitted Mere and Blessing Pres-ence (Which is generally Given via His Agencies and Instruments), all devotees will always be Awakened to the Revelation of the Divine Person, the Self-Existing and Self-Radiant Consciousness Who lives as all beings and animates all conditions. Because Heart-Master Da has been born, Incarnating the Divine Person in our time, men and women now (and in the future) have the unequaled opportunity to understand themselves and to Realize the Way of Grace that has been Initiated and Revealed in His Liberating Company.

The talks and essays in this book reveal what devotees in moments of Enlightened Intuition have seen: Heart-Master Da is the Very Self of all, the One Consciousness by Whose Power and Grace even ordinary men and women may be forever Liberated from bondage to this world of fleeting pleasures and certain pain. Heart-Master Da is none other than the One Being Who Lives as every being, freely Giving the most precious Gift to all, Gracefully showering all beings with True Understanding and Infinite Joy. He is the Teacher of those who gratefully receive His Word of Truth and embrace the ordeal of self-understanding, and He is the True Heart-Master of those who, having understood, surrender in His Mere and Blessing Presence of Love, and who thereby receive, in the paradox of Devotional Submission, the Grace of Perfect Freedom. May every heart Awaken to His Sign of Realization, which communicates to all the Condition of inherent Freedom and Happiness. He is, as His Name signals, the "Giver of Love-Bliss", and He has Given in abundance all the Gifts necessary to Awaken every heart. How the Way of the Heart now unfolds for any man or woman depends on his or her reception and response.

FOR THE READER

THIS BOOK

The Spiritual and functional practices and disciplines discussed in this book, including the meditative practices, the Yogic exercises of "conductivity", the breathing exercises, the life-disciplines of right diet and exercise, the intelligent economization and practice of sexuality, etc., are appropriate and natural practices that are voluntarily and progressively adopted by each practicing member of The Free Daist Communion and adapted to his or her personal circumstance. Although anyone may find them useful and beneficial, they are not presented as advice or recommendations to the general reader or to anyone who is not a practicing member of The Free Daist Communion. And nothing in this book is intended as a diagnosis, prescription, or recommended treatment or cure for any specific "problem", whether medical, emotional, psychological, social, or Spiritual. One should apply a particular program of treatment, prevention, cure, or general health only in consultation with a licensed physician or other qualified professional.

AN INVITATION TO RESPONSIBILITY

The Way of the Heart that Heart-Master Da has Revealed is an invitation to everyone to assume real responsibility for his or her life. As Heart-Master Da has said in *The Dawn Horse Testament*, "If any one Is Interested In The Realization Of The Heart, Let him or her First Submit To Be Taught Through The Ordeal Of self-Observation, self-Enquiry, self-Understanding, and self-Transcendence." Therefore, participation in the Way of the Heart requires a real struggle with oneself, and not at all a struggle with Heart-Master Da, or with others.

All who study the Way of the Heart or take up its practice should remember that they are responding to a call to become responsible for themselves, and they should understand that they, not Heart-Master

Da, are responsible for any decision they may make or action they may take in the course of their lives of study or practice. This has always been true, and it is true whatever the individual's involvement in the Way of the Heart, be it as reader, student, beginning practitioner, or devotee.

HEART-MASTER DA AND HIS INSTRUMENTS AND SPIRITUAL AGENCIES

At times Heart-Master Da speaks or writes of having "Agency" or "Instruments". He uses the words "Agency" and "Instrument" strictly in the Spiritual sense rather than in any temporal or worldly sense. He uses the word "Agency" to denote the capacity for magnifying His Transmission of the Perfectly Enlightened Condition, while the word "Instrumentality" indicates the capacity for magnifying Heart-Master Da's Revelation and Spiritual Blessing in the stages of life and practice previous to Divine Enlightenment. While all true practitioners of the Way of the Heart act as Instruments to one or another degree through their reception and honoring of the Gifts Heart-Master Da has given, advanced practitioners (through their real Spiritual reception of Heart-Blessing, rather than through any self-conscious or independent intention) function naturally as Spiritual Instruments for Heart-Master Da's spontaneous Transmission of Heart-Blessing.

At the time this book is published the principal means of Heart-Master Da's Agency and Instrumentality are the Wisdom-Teaching of the Way of the Heart and the Sanctuaries Empowered by Him. He does not yet have "human Agency", that is, individuals whose Perfect Awakening has moved Him to acknowledge them as His Agency, though there may come a time when Heart-Master Da acknowledges such human Spiritual Agency.

All should also understand that neither The Free Daist Communion nor any of its representatives or members "represents" Heart-Master Da, either in the temporal sense, as His agent, or in the Spiritual sense, as His Agent. Heart-Master Da is a legal renunciate of the Communion. Therefore, the Communion provides a living circumstance for Him and is authorized to publish His writings. But Heart-Master Da functions only Spiritually, and in Freedom. For many years He has owned nothing and has had no worldly responsibilities and has exercised no worldly functions. He has been and is a true renunciate. He has not directed and does not direct in any way any of the activities of the Communion or of its representatives or members. Therefore, Heart-Master Da is not responsible for any of the activities of the Communion, its representatives, or its members.

LOOK AT THE SUNLIGHT ON THE WATER

Educating Children for a Life of
Self-Transcending Love and Happiness

HEART-MASTER DA

(The Avadhoota Da Love-Ananda Hridayam,
Whose Teaching Name Is Da Free John)

Note: When this 1983 edition of *Look at the Sunlight on the Water* was published, Heart-Master Da was known as Da Free John. The main text of this book is simply a reprint of the 1983 edition, and therefore the reader will find the name "Da Free John" used throughout.

INTRODUCTION

by Georg Feuerstein

1979 was declared, by United Nations idealists, the Year of the Child. However, the unforeseen sensation over the American hostages in Iran stole the headlines—a telling commentary on the priorities of mass culture. What, one may ask, is so special about the child? Politicians and economists (who, after all, run our civilization) have a ready answer to this question: Ever since the Industrial Revolution, when young children were forced to sell the scant strength of their still-developing muscles for a pittance to supplement the income of their families, the child has been recognized as a valuable asset to a country's economy. Though child labor is largely eradicated and certainly outlawed in the "developed" nations, the educated child is nonetheless considered a precious investment. The United States government alone spends annually around $80,000,000,000 to educate its young citizens between the ages of five and seventeen. This is eighty billion dollars more than was spent on education in the whole millennia-long history of our earliest ancestors in the Paleolithic.

At the dawn of human history, or more accurately prehistory, life itself was the only school. Our hunting-and-gathering forebears (and their children) mostly learned the hard way: by trial and error. Certain rudimentary skills and "useful" attitudes were passed on informally from adult to child. Perhaps a gentle cuff or jab for a slow learner was all there was to "formal" education. Education was part of the program of spontaneous socialization within the horde or clan. Conformism was natural since there were no cultural alternatives to cause conflict and deviance. Members of the Stone Age clan were carbon copies of each other—ideal subjects of any totalitarian regime. However, although our ancestors were well adapted to their environment, their skills and possibly their intelligence would be barely sufficient for survival in the highly artificial environment of the twentieth century.

Our Neolithic ancestors might do somewhat better in this respect. As settled farmers, they created the economic surplus to give birth to urban environs with their increasing division of labor and inevitable bureaucracy. They had to put a premium on learning in a more formal way to maintain the complexity of a sedentary way of life. But this threw them into an immediate conflict: the learning that guaranteed socioeconomic stability in the new setting was also a potential danger to the established way of life, because it opened up new perspectives. Knowledge was thus recognized to be a great power—and a threat. Therefore, it became the almost exclusive property of a privileged minority—the political-religious elite. This was the way in the primary cultures of Sumer, Egypt, and India, as well as in the later cultures of Greece and Rome, and not least in Europe during the Middle Ages.

Nor has this monopolizing tendency died out, though today's knowledge-manipulators are more subtle about the ways in which they grant the masses access to knowledge. Today, the cognitive straitjackets are put on early in life. This is done by the curriculum of the school and even university (the "brain factory"). Indoctrination is another word for this process. In a way, the modern mass education encourages the kind of conformism that was natural to our Stone Age ancestors but that is atavistic and soul-destroying today, at a time in the evolution of human consciousness when individuality should not be levelled but transcended. This tendency toward mass-produced uniformity is not only immoral, it is also impractical. The clock cannot be turned back, at least not without also reducing human civilization to its original primitivity. Individuality is the psychological matrix that shapes our civilization—its ceaseless creativity, relative openness, and unparalleled self-transforming capacity. To encourage further the present trend toward "equalization" or "standardization" of human behavior is, therefore, dangerous. For, "hollow people," the psychologically impotent, are incapable of facing the complexities of our present society, never mind the global world of the future. Human cogwheels cannot drive the machinery of our postmodern civilization. Cybernetic brains would be far more efficient and economic.

Luckily, our troubled civilization is sufficiently self-reflective to recognize that a change is urgently called for in just about every area of life, but not least in education. Countless diagnoses of our situation are piled up every year, and equally many remedies are suggested by educators, psychologists, historians, and philosophers. Unfortunately, there is no unanimity of answers; there is no generally agreed-upon anthropology, or Image of Man. Yet, such an Image is crucial to education and to the new world-view or understanding of reality that must emerge in order to usher Man into the twenty-first century without the crippling fear of impending self-annihilation through ecological catastrophe or global war.

While educators are fumbling in the dark for definitive "models" and "systems" and "programs," they are experimenting on the adults of the next millennium, and our children continue to be molded into personalities that are unlikely to be able to cope with the future. More importantly, though, they are educated below their human potential. And by "potential" is not meant merely their hidden creativity, bodily talent, intellectual and moral capability, or their capacity for well-adapted interpersonal relations. As Abraham Maslow, the visionary doyen of "humanistic psychology," saw and fearlessly propagandized, full humanness includes the ability to transcend the self. In fact, it presupposes active self-transcendence. What this means, in the last analysis, is abiding in the disposition of Transcendental Realization. For, when the self is transcended, Reality shines forth as it is, without the distortions introduced by the self-referring egoic entity. This capacity of the human being to Ecstatically step beyond his presumed skin-wrapped identity is his *spiritual* potential.

Yet, the modern knowledge industry—which Ivan Illich, archcritic of contemporary education, styled the "New World Church"—is disturbingly oblivious of this dimension of human existence. And even in those elect circles where the need for an alternative education is enduring table talk, spiritual values and the high art of self-transcendence receive second billing after consciousness-raising techniques, self-actualizing therapies, and personal growth philosophies. This is hardly surprising: Our cultural leaders have little or no acquaintance with spiritual life. They have been milled through much the same bland secular education that is now tailoring their children to the needs of our technological society.

As Ivan Illich, Paul Goodman, Everett Reimer, and others have made clear, formal schooling is neither the only nor the most effective way of educating our children. Fortunately, schools are a dying race of dinosaurs. But the proposed learning networks, personalized (and lifetime) education, problem-solving orientation, and computer-assisted self-learning, and so forth, are also no panacea. They may have a mildly balancing effect on the roller coaster of the knowledge explosion and postindustrial development, but in themselves they will not suffice to create the necessary ethos for the global society of the twenty-first century. Education is form *and* content. Now, if education is seen as the means by which the individual learns to participate in the realities of the larger society, then those realities must be clearly understood. And here the bottom line is that the realities of conventional life are the realities of billions of beings suffering from what Abraham Maslow dubbed the "Jonah complex": the fearful evasion of one's highest possibilities, the anxious self-denial of a destiny "larger than life." Ultimately, of course, Maslow's "Jonah complex" is the egoic recoil from Reality itself. This has been most cogently articulated by the Adept Da Free John:

> *Birth is shock. It is the primal incident. As an incident, it is usually interpreted psychologically—in terms of its emotional-mental or subjective impact. But its significance is in the event itself, the sudden event of existence as the whole body. Birth is itself shock—vital shock, a recoil at Infinity. Our life is a drama of subjective struggling against an unbearable demand: relationship, incarnation, or love. We are in the mood of recoil, contraction, and self-possession—not by virtue of some inward and soulish pre-existence, but by virtue of birth itself, the apparent independence of self all relationships imply.*[1]

Part of the problem with schools is that they represent an artificial environment that, moreover, is out of sync with the learning environment within the home and the larger community. But even within that wider, natural context, learning is narrowly focused on mechanical and intellectual skills and rarely on emotional growth, never mind *spiritual* maturation. Nor can conventional religious education, in and out of school, be said to plumb the spiritual depth of

---

1. Bubba [Da] Free John, *The Paradox of Instruction,* rev. ed. (1977), p. 39.

human existence and awaken the child to the dimension of Reality, or what Master Da Free John calls the "Radiant Transcendental Being." Yet, without such a spiritual awakening of the being, true humanness is unrealizable. To become truly human, Man must transcend what he seems to be. He must make the leap—a quite paradoxical vault—beyond the conventional image of himself and of the world, an image that essentially transfixes him to the pseudo-human existence that, today, threatens our species with extinction. Full humanness is coincident with perfect self-transcendence, or Enlightened or God-Realized existence.

Clearly, education must go beyond the humanist curriculum that we inherited from Greece and Rome via the Renaissance. It must likewise go beyond the religious fundamentalism that was ripe in the Medieval period, dominated as it was by the otherworldly dogmatism of Christianity (stifling cultural development). It must go beyond the secularized, science-oriented liberal education that has its roots in the liberalizing idealism of the seventeenth century and that, under the growing influence of the technologization of society, has become more and more utilitarian and materialistic. It must definitely go beyond the modern outgrowth of this trend: vocational training, or the molding of individuals into compliant tools of industry and commerce. This reduction of education to mere skill training is one of the most lamentable and pernicious consequences of scientistic ideology, which together with religious provincialism is a major evil of our time. Master Da Free John, raising the prophetic voice of the Realized Adept, speaks of them as the two great "heresies" that obstruct the higher evolutionary destiny of mankind.

Thus, education must go beyond the Socratic ideal of the virtuous or good man, beyond the Enlightenment ideal of the rational and knowledgeable person, beyond the conventional religious ideal of the God-fearing soul, as well as beyond the postmodern ideal (if it deserves the status of an ideal at all) of the competent or useful citizen. It must even go beyond the human potential ideal of the perpetual, happy actualizer or learner. The last-mentioned viewpoint is represented in a masterly manner by G. B. Leonard who, in his widely acclaimed book *Education and Ecstasy,* professes that "learning itself is life's ultimate purpose" (p. 216). It is true that joy is a better "reinforcer" for learning than punishment. It is also more "human" to spend one's life "in the joyful pursuit of learning" (p. 230) than to be submotivated by fear, anger, greed, or jealousy. Yet, self-transcendence does not stop at confessions of exuberance or joy. Genuine Ecstasy transcends the mental-emotional dimension. It is coessential with the Transcendental Reality itself. The *ananda* (Sanskrit: "bliss") which Leonard lauds so highly is not a human emotion. It is literally a Blissful "standing outside" (*ek-stasis*) of oneself.

What would education be if perfect self-transcendence were acknowledged as the supreme value of human existence? What would human life be if Man were viewed from the vantage-point of his Transcendental Identity rather than his multiple egoic identities or role-playing personas? How would the world look if Enlightenment were recognized as the principle of existence? What would be the shape of a whole community, or society, of self-transcending and God-Realized beings who "are the unexploitable Presence of Reality"?[2] Master Da Free John, whose declared purpose is to create a seed community of such Enlightened beings, answers these questions in principle thus.

[*Such beings*] *will not devote themselves to turning the world to dilemma, exhaustion, and revolutionary experience, nor to the degenerative exploitation of desire and possibility, nor to the ascent to and inclusion of various illusory goals, higher entities, evolutionary aims, or deluded ideas of experiential transformation. They will create in the aesthetics of Reality, turning all things into radical relationship and enjoyment. They will remove the effects of separative existence and restore the Form of things. They will engineer every kind of stability and beauty. They will create a Presence of Peace. Their eye will be on present form and not on exaggerated notions of artifice. Their idea of form is stable and whole, not a gesture toward some other event. They will not make the world seem but a symbol for higher and other things.*

They will constantly create the form of Truth while conscious of Present Reality. Thus, they will serve the order of sacrifice and

2. Da Free John, *Scientific Proof of the Existence of God Will Soon Be Announced by the White House!* p. 110.

*liberated knowledge. They will evolve the necessary and good, and
make economic and wise use of all technology. They will not be
motivated by invention but by Reality, which is the Presence to be
communicated in all forms. They will not pursue any kind of false
victory, any fearful deathlessness or overwhelming survival for Man.
They will only create the conditions for present enjoyment, the
communication of Reality, the Form in which understanding can arise,
live, and become the public foundation of existence.*[3]

Utopianism? Only insofar as this vision has "no place" (*ou
topos*) as yet in the larger society. However, it has become reality in
the growing community of spiritual practitioners of Master Da Free
John's Way of Radical Understanding: in the spring and summer of
1983, several practitioners transitioned into the disposition of
Enlightenment—a small beginning, but a beginning nonetheless. The
fact that there is now, after eleven years of intensive Teaching on the
part of Master Da Free John, a nucleus of men and women who are
firmly established in the Bliss of Transcendental Consciousness
verifies the validity of the Way taught by this great Adept. It also lends
credence to his basic anthropology and model of education, as
formulated in the unique framework of the "seven stages of life."

The seven stages of life represent a comprehensive phenomeno-
logical map of individual (and, potentially, species-wide) human
development from the biological event of birth to the spiritual event
of full Enlightenment, or Awakening in the seventh stage of life. By
comparison, the developmental models of modern psychology are
exclusive of higher human maturation, anchored as they are in a
preeminently materialistic worldview. Also, these models are largely
confined to childhood and adolescence, though some include the
"second puberty" of the climacterium (middle age) into their periodization of human life. The developmental models current in the great
religious traditions, notably Hinduism, while taking Man's spiritual
maturation into account, nevertheless lack the radical point of view.
So, instead of being based on the presumption of Man's prior
Enlightenment (or the highest evolutionary possibility), they operate
with a model of gradual progression toward what is conceived as the

3. Ibid., pp. 110-11.

goal of Liberation. The development of the individual is accordingly viewed as a vertical movement away from the problematic existential situation (interpreted as a hoard of suffering and sorrow) and toward the solution of a disposition of superiority over the world. The path is seen as the realization of an ascetical, life-negative metaphysics.

The idea that human life proceeds in distinct stages is obviously rooted in experience. Similarly, the periodization into phases of seven years (for the first three stages) is not as arbitrary as it may seem. In the Western world, seven-year cycles of personal growth were first suggested by Solon (600 B.C.), the Athenian lawgiver. Around the time of Jesus of Nazareth the idea was renewedly propounded by the Jewish philosopher Philo, and in the Middle Ages the notion was revived among Christian and Moslem scholastics. Modern theories perceive different discontinuities in the maturation process, and the divergence between these models is explained by their varying range of orientation, comprehensiveness, and purpose.[4]

The basis for Master Da Free John's model of the seven stages of life is simply the Adept's acute observation of human behavior and experience, not only within the realm of ordinary or conventional existence but within the dimension of extraordinary manifestations of consciousness and capacity. His framework is, like his approach in general, an expression of his keen sense for the essential and practically useful. Thus, the seven stages of life are, in principle, seven lessons or seven approaches and opportunities to learn the lesson of life. Each phase is not only a new dimension of life experience but also a new life theme or area of obligation or responsibility which calls for application and mastery.

Each stage unfolds according to its own inner logic. The first three stages are semiautonomous, whereas in the next three stages, maturation is primarily determined by the voluntary practice of self-transcendence. In the final or seventh stage of life, pure spontaneity replaces both biological determinism and conscious effort. In a way, the underlying theme of the first three stages can be said to be the development or formation of the individual into a maturely functioning human being.

Thus, in the first stage the young child learns "simple" skills, like

---

4. See the theories of development by S. Freud, J. Piaget, C. Bühler, E. Erikson, and others.

focusing with the eyes, grasping and manipulating objects, assimilating and converting food and breath into energy, walking, talking, controlling bladder and bowels, relating to his fellow beings, and, toward the end of the stage, somewhat more abstract thinking.

The second stage of life is the phase in which the growing child matures in its emotional-sexual nature and learns to integrate and coordinate its inner life with the gross physical dimension. The young personality grows in his self-awareness as a social being in an ever-expanding sphere of relations. Just as in the first stage one learns about and becomes responsible for the assimilation and elimination of elemental food, in the second stage one must likewise learn about and adapt to a new form of sustenance: emotional-social interaction. The sexual awakening that occurs in this phase is coincident with the accelerated development of the glandular and hormonal system of the body. It is vitally important that sexual maturation and emotional maturation should be synchronized and integrated with each other. Failure to accomplish harmonious emotional-sexual development results in the usual hard-to-remedy adult neuroses.

The third stage of life is the stage of the maturation of the intellect and will and of the integration of the vital-physical, emotional-sexual, and mental-intentional functions. This stage marks the transition to full individuation, wherein the first two stages of life are adapted to a practical and analytical intelligence and an informed will or intention. Here the individual will have a clear self-image and be capable of relating functionally to the world.

Considering that the fully functional or well-adapted individual is the goal of such corrective approaches as psychoanalysis, psychotherapy, and many of the "third force" psychological schools, our society consists largely of individuals who have failed to achieve ordinary maturity at the termination of the third stage of life. As Master Da Free John observes:

There is commonly a lag in the transition to manhood, man or woman, because of the shocks experienced in the immature attempts to function in the world. Thus, to some degree, every man or woman lingers in the childhood assumption of dependence.[5]

5. Da Free John, *Scientific Proof of the Existence of God Will Soon Be Announced by the White House!* p. 38.

There must be a transition from childhood to maturity. That transition is also commonly acknowledged as a stage in the psycho-physical development of a human being. It is called adolescence. This stage also tends to be prolonged indefinitely, and, indeed, perhaps the majority of "civilized" men and women are occupied with the concerns of this transition most of their lives.[6]

As was indicated earlier, the functional individual does not yet embody full humanness. "The truly human being," as Master Da Free John explains, "appears only in the fourth stage of life."[7] Here, the individual consciously submits to the spiritual process by way of heartfelt surrender to, and intuition of, the Transcendental Reality or Being-Consciousness. This process continues until, in the seventh stage of life, there is a *Gestalt* switch from the empirical or personal identity to the Transcendental Identity—the ultimate fulfillment of the lifelong process of spiritual education or schooling.

When viewed in the light of this Way of life, which is the actualization of Man's *total* potential, the education of children assumes singular importance. It is the foundation for the spiritual process itself. Conventional socialization and education are quite incapable of promoting the growth of healthy, well-adapted, self-actualizing individuals, not to mention individuals motivated toward self-transcendence. The dilemmas and struggles faced by adult practitioners of the Way of Radical Understanding (and other spiritual approaches!) are principally the result of the failure of their social and educational environment. But these inner difficulties are wholly unnecessary. Neurotic maladaptations to life, especially emotional retardation, need not continue to be the stumbling blocks that prevent adults from engaging the spiritual process effectively. They can be obviated by a childhood education that is based on the recognition of Man as a being capacitated for self-transcendence and ultimate God-Realization.

6. Ibid., p. 39.

7. Bubba [Da] Free John, *Love of the Two-Armed Form,* p. 75.

To create an educational environment in which such preparation for authentic spiritual life is made possible has been one of the goals of the community of practitioners of the Way of Radical Understanding. In fact, it is being increasingly recognized that, in a self-transcending community of this type, the education of children is an integral part of spiritual practice itself. The community is a comprehensive learning environment in which all practitioners—adults and children alike—are related to each other in a dialectics of mutual education. For, responsibility for the education (that is, for the rudimentary spiritual practice) of children can only be truly met when the adults are responsible in their own application to the process of self-transcendence. Thus, children and adults make a (spoken or unspoken) demand on each other for spiritual practice and in this manner constantly embody the spiritual anthropology of this Way of life. The children's culture is seen to develop in direct relationship to the maturation of the community as a whole—a slow process but one whose ultimate possibilities are of such magnitude that they exceed the imagination of even the practitioners who are involved in this great experiment. In the past, the pursuit of Enlightenment has always been the occupation of a select few who, as a rule, abandoned the world or who at least created their own cultural enclaves in the shape of ashrams and monasteries. Although great Adepts like Gautama the Buddha and the Tibetan Master Padmasambhava are said to have left behind small groups of Enlightened beings, these did not form true communities because of the absence of family life, dictated by the monastic ideal.

By contrast, the community envisioned by the Adept Da Free John is fully integrated with the technological world at large, yet brings to it a different value system, in fact a different kind of human being. The operative principle is relationship, not dissociation or sectarian exclusivism on the one hand or world-conquering reformism on the other. Step by arduous step, this grand vision is being translated into reality by a small but rapidly growing community of practitioners of the Way of Radical Understanding. Through his incessant demands for active self-transcendence, Master Da Free John keeps this vision firmly before everyone's eyes.

Out of the cloud of Compassion
The rain of the Doctrine of the Victorious One
Falls without premeditation
As a continuous harvest for all.[8]

This slender volume is an introduction to Master Da Free John's wisdom on children's education in the context of his larger spiritual Teaching. The basic argument of Master Da Free John's Way of Radical Understanding or Divine Ignorance derives from the insights that informed his own spiritual practice and that became crystallized and ultimately confirmed in the event of his full Enlightenment on September 10, 1970. However, in its extended form, his Teaching, including his wisdom on education and his book for children entitled *What to Remember to Be Happy,* represents a spontaneous development, occurring in response to the spiritual needs of the community of practitioners of his Way. His Teaching is not an intellectual effort at systematizing knowledge about the spiritual process, but a living consideration, carried by the perfect spontaneity that is the essence of the Enlightened disposition. Much of Master Da Free John's Teaching is, therefore, contained in his talks with practitioners in which he spontaneously sheds light on specific situations, though never without placing any given issue into the general context of spiritual practice in the radical sense.

Most of the talks appearing in this book specifically present Master Da's Wisdom Teaching on the ideal design for an "ashram school"[9] for children in the third stage of life (ages 12-21 years).

This book contains materials of practical relevance for teachers and parents both within and outside the community of spiritual practitioners who apply this radical education. It should be self-evident from what has been said above that the following talks and essays are not merely about schooling, or about children. Rather, they are about a new Way of life in which the principle of human growth and human interaction is "radical understanding."

---

8. Sgam.po.pa's *The Jewel Ornament of Liberation,* ch. XXI. Translated from the Tibetan by H. von Guenther (London: Rider, 1970), p. 273.

9. An ashram is a place where a Spiritual Master gathers the community of his devotees in order to live with them, instruct them, and communicate the Living Force of his Presence. Master Da Free John sometimes uses the term to include the entire community or fellowship of devotees,

This radical understanding is the only real Liberation, and it alone is the Truth and Realization of this moment. Every motive is seeking. Every turning away is avoidance. Every turning upwards is avoidance. Every turning downwards is avoidance. Every turning towards is avoidance. All these things are seeking, for they are not abiding now in the Form of Reality. Thus, to turn at all is to act. And every turning will awaken the reaction of turning the opposite way in time.

The Truth is radical non-avoidance moment to moment. It is to live this moment, this event, without conflict, directly. Where there is understanding there is no turning, and every action turns no way at all, for there is only radical Consciousness behind it, turning no way, knowing only great Bliss.[10]

The talks and essays in this volume are an Adept's Enlightened consideration on education, especially the education of teenagers, and an invitation to teachers and parents to offer children the unique opportunity of growing into fully mature beings who value and practice the art of self-transcendence.

wherever they may be located. An "ashram school," which is a community-founded and community-operated endeavor, combines the intimate living circumstance of an ashram with the spiritual, cultural, and academic education for children in the third stage of life.

10. Bubba [Da] Free John, *The Knee of Listening*, p. 225.

PART I

HUMAN LIFE AS A PROCESS OF GROWTH

INTRODUCTION TO PART I

This first chapter consists of a lengthy talk in which Master Da Free John reads, as is his custom, a new essay to a small gathering of practitioners, commenting on it wherever he feels further explanation may clarify his intent.

In his discussion, Master Da Free John focuses on the first three stages of life, covering the period from birth to the twenty-first year. He particularly elaborates on the critical second stage (seven to fourteen), in which the individual begins to, or at least should begin to, awaken in his emotional and feeling being. In the first stage of life, education is basically designed to facilitate the process of individuation which, when fulfilled, makes the child available for the key considerations and demands of the second stage. It is in the second stage that the groundwork for later spiritual practice is laid. Having learned the fact of his physical independence in the first stage, the second-stage child learns to experience himself as actually being connected to others and to his surroundings on the level of energy.

He is thus educated to move beyond the cultural lag that still separates the majority of adults from the revolutionary findings of modern physics: namely, that the stability of our everyday reality is mere appearance. The universe is an unimaginably vast sea of matter-energy, of which matter is simply a particular (or particularly congealed) state, and energy another. However, neither is ultimate. Rather, both inhere in, or are modifications of, the Transcendental Being-Consciousness—as will become obvious when the spiritual process has matured sufficiently.

On the basis of his firsthand experience of the energetic dimension of life, the child learns to assume responsibility for his psycho-mental states, since these are reflected in his energy field in its interaction with other fields. Environmental pollution is thus not only a matter of spoiling air, land, and sea. It is also, and perhaps more so, a matter of corrupting the total energy field of our life-world by reactive emotions and physical disequilibrium, and thereby affecting others negatively in their emotional and physical life. This thought itself is not new, though it never has had the corroboration of science. What is new is that this insight is integrated into an educational curriculum.

A large portion of Master Da Free John's exhortative talk concerns sexuality—one of the great problem areas of contemporary life. Though not endorsing the sex-negative, repressive stance of most traditional religious paths, the Adept nevertheless regards sexual discipline (in the form of sexual conservation) as a necessity of the educational process in the first three stages. The reason for this is that sexual energy is closely associated with the Life-Energy of the body and that the proper conduction of this Force is instrumental not only to personal growth but the later spiritual process. Of course, this approach to sexual education is almost entirely dependent on a confessed attitude in children, which presupposes a relationship of intimacy. But such intimacy is only possible if both children and adults are sensitive to each other and actively participate, in the forms appropriate to them, in the wider spiritual culture.

As will become obvious from Master Da Free John's illuminating treatment of the third stage of life, the energy dimension with which second-stage children should become most familiar is only one aspect of our "subtle" being. The human being is a multidimensional process—an understanding that has long been the exclusive property of the esoteric traditions but that science is in the process of rediscovering for the generations of the next millennium. For Master Da Free John, education is the literal enlargement of the child's (and adult's) horizon of experience, whereby the learning individual is gradually introduced to dimensions of existence which lie beyond the mere physical and which are ignored in secular (materialistic) education.

However, although this extension of the individual's experiential capacity leads to a fuller and more human life, Master Da Free John never tires of pointing out that a much greater destiny awaits the whole or sane human being: the ultimate transcendence of what is typically human or egoic existence. It is this radical point of view that alone is able to sustain the momentum of the schooling in the first six stages of life.

Come to the edge, he said.
They said: We are afraid.
Come to the edge, he said.
They came.
He pushed them . . . and they flew.[1]

1. The poem is by Guillaume Apollinaire. Quoted by M. Ferguson, *The Aquarian Conspiracy: Personal and Social Transformation in the 1980s* (Los Angeles: J. P. Tarcher, 1980), p. 293.

Chapter 1

Education, or My Way of Schooling in the Seven Stages of Life

an essay with commentary by Da Free John
March 1, 1983

M ASTER DA FREE JOHN: The essay I am about to read is called "Education, or My Way of Schooling in the Seven Stages of Life."

Each of the seven stages represents a unique period of adaptation and transcendence, and each subsequent stage is built upon fulfillment of the process of adaptation and transcendence in all previous stages. Therefore, we must clearly understand what special education or schooling must be engaged in each stage.

The remainder of the essay describes these requirements stage by stage. Before going on, however, I want to emphasize the statement, "each subsequent stage is built upon fulfillment of the process of adaptation and transcendence in all previous stages." If you do not fulfill a stage before proceeding to the next one, then there will be complications, and any attempt at future growth will in effect be retarded. This is true both in the first three stages, the adaptation to so-called ordinary life, and in the later stages, which principally pertain to spiritual life.

The essay goes on to consider the first stage:

Stage 1: This is the stage that basically occupies us from conception to seven years of age (or the beginning of true socialization and complex relatedness). It is the period in which we must adapt to our physical individuality and basic physical capacity. Thus, it is not only a period of physical adaptation, but of physical individuation. That is, we must gradually adapt to fully functional physical existence, but we must achieve physical individuation, or physical (and thus mental, emotional, psychic, and psychological) independence from the mother and all others. When this stage is complete, we will not exist in isolation but in a state of conscious relatedness to all others and the world of Nature. Thus, the fulfillment of the first stage of life is marked by the beginnings of the movement toward more complex socialization, cooperation with others, and sensitivity to the total world of Nature.

The first stage of life is basically the period of physical adaptation to our functional existence, though other forms of adaptation begin to occur as physical adaptation matures. In addition to the obvious process of physical adaptation, what must also occur at this stage is physical individuation. This means that the child in the first stage of life must realize that he or she is an independent physical personality. In other words, he or she must break the dependency connection to the mother. This is a kind of unconscious connection to another being in which nurturing occurs. The individual must achieve physical independence and therefore mental and emotional independence from the mother.

It is only on the basis of individuation from this one-on-one bond—or more to the point, this "two-who-are-one" bond—that the individual can move out socially, into the whole field of relationships. The first stage is complete when we can see the beginnings of a movement toward a more complex socialization with adults and peers, and toward cooperation with others and sensitivity to the total world of Nature.

I should also indicate that the stages of life overlap one another. There are seven stages of life, but there is a period of time at the end of each of the first six stages wherein some characteristics and capabilities of the next stage begin to appear. Thus, toward the end of the first stage of life we should expect to see the signs of individuation, socialization, cooperation, sensitivity to Nature, and so forth. When these signs show themselves stably and significantly, then the schooling of the second stage of life becomes appropriate and inevitable.

The essay goes on to talk about the second stage as follows:

> Stage 2: The second stage of life is the early stage (particularly occupying us during the second seven years of life) of adaptation to the etheric dimension of our manifest existence. The etheric dimension may be functionally described as the emotional-sexual dimension of our being, but it is in essence the dimension of energy, nerve-force, and direct feeling-sensitivity to the conditions of existence. Since the second stage is the primary stage of socialization, we can say that it is the basic stage of moral or right relational development. But the primary adaptation is to feeling, or sensitivity to the energy inherent in one's person, and which is in all others, and which pervades all of Nature. Thus, this stage is not merely the stage of conventional socialization, but it is the stage in which feeling-sensitivity is developed relative to one's own etheric dimension (or energy field),[1] that of others, and that which is everywhere. When this feeling-sensitivity is exercised, one learns that one is more than merely physical, but one is also a field of energy that extends to others and communicates emotional, mental, psychic, and physical states to others as well as to the natural world. Therefore, one must learn to be responsible for one's emotional, mental, psychic, and physical state by participating in or surrendering

---

1. "The etheric dimension of force or manifest light pervades and surrounds our universe and every physical body. It is the field of energy, magnetism, and space in which the lower or grosser elements function. Thus, your 'etheric body' is the specific concentration of force associated with and surrounding-permeating your physical body. It serves as a conduit for the forces of universal light and energy to the physical body.

"In practical terms of daily experience, the etheric aspect of the being is our emotional-sexual, feeling nature. The etheric body functions through and corresponds to the nervous system. Functioning as a medium between the conscious mind and the physical being, it controls the distribution and use of energy and emotion. It is the dimension of vitality or life-force. We feel the etheric dimension of life not only as vital energy and power and magnetic-gravitational forces, but also as the endless play of emotional polarization, positive and negative, to others, objects, the world itself, everything that arises" (Da Free John, *Conscious Exercise and the Transcendental Sun*, pp. 27–28).

openly into the domains of Life-Energy. By doing this, one's social development and one's involvement in the natural world will develop as a moral and feeling gesture, rather than an amoral (or self-possessed and other-manipulative) form of conventional socialization and worldliness.

The schooling of the second stage of life is not directly sexual. Genital sexuality and social patterns of a demonstratively sexual nature should be conserved, or by-passed through right understanding, until the third stage of life is complete—in order that we may first develop full human responsibility for what must become the yoga of sexual communion.[2] But the learning in the second stage of life should provide the living emotional base (and balance) for later sexual activity.

The training in the second stage of life should involve exercises that develop sensitivity to the etheric or energy field of the body-mind. Practices such as the laying on of hands[3] and general physical and emotional sensitivity to the livingness and feelings of others should be developed. This stage is complete when the individual has achieved a basic level of social individuation—so that he or she no longer requires the parent-child style of relationship, but can freely and rightly and responsibly associate with the larger world of adults and peers. Thus, a child's movement into the third stage of life should be formally acknowledged by the parents, who must then relinquish any residual interest in binding the child to the parent-child style of relationship. Instead, the child should move into the third stage of life as a socially individuated person, responsible to the larger

2. "Sexual communion" is the technical term used by Master Da Free John to describe the natural practice of human emotional and sexual intimacy between lovers wherein body, mind, self-sense, the loved one, and the sexual experience itself are surrendered in direct Communion with the All-Pervading Divine. For a detailed treatment of this aspect of spiritual practice, see *Love of the Two-Armed Form*, by Da Free John.

3. The laying on of hands, an aid to healing others through release of all conditions to the Divine and radiation of the Power of Life, is generally performed on an intimate's behalf, often while maintaining physical contact via the hands. See *The Eating Gorilla Comes in Peace*, by Da Free John, pp. 462–70, for a complete description.

community of adults (including his or her parents) as a non-child, or a socially responsible young person. In that case, the third stage of life will not be characterized by adolescent ambivalence, cycling back and forth between the separate motives of dependence and independence, but it will be characterized by the steady growth of an individuated but relationally positive person.

Just as the first stage of life has been fulfilled when the individual has realized a state of physical individuation and therefore has become capable of social existence and an expanded feeling association with Nature and in all relationships, the second stage of life is fulfilled when the individual has realized a state of social individuation. In other words, the individual is free, not merely of the unconscious bond to the mother, but free of the parent-child style of relationship altogether. He or she can function as a socially independent or free individual responsible to the adult community. He or she is not yet an adult, or a person who can go into the world and do what he or she wants, but rather he or she is a physically and socially individuated person who is responsible to and is to be guided by the adult community.

The other important point made in the essay about the second stage of life relates to this matter of etheric sensitivity. The second stage of life, apart from the process of socialization, is the school in which we develop our feeling-sensitivity. In other words, we develop the capacity of the etheric being, or the being who is not just a physical personality, but who is a force that is manifested as a field of energy in contact with the energies of Nature and the Universal Energy Field in which Nature is arising. In order to allow this whole process of feeling-sensitivity to mature, the individual must discover that he or she is just such an etheric or energy-based personality.

When we see a baby, it is obvious to us that it is a physically independent personality, but the baby is not consciously aware of precisely what this physical individuation is about and how he or she is different from the mother and others. This sense of physical individuation develops through a learning process that occurs during infancy and in the early years of childhood. This learning process eventually results in a clear sense of individuation, physical capacity, and a sense of relatedness to others, including the parents, other adults, and the world in general. It is not immediately obvious to an infant that it is a physical individual or separate physical personality. Likewise, it is not readily obvious to young people, or even to many adults who have never really undergone the true learning of the second stage of life, that they are manifested as an energy field. This must be learned through self-observation and self-exercise. Thus, our initial guidance of a young child—and some of this training can begin even in the first stage of life—would include helping the child to become aware of his own energy field.

The process whereby we achieve sensitivity to this energy field is through the primary sense of touch, or through feeling contact. The other senses may play a part in this sensitivity to or observation of the energy field, but the primary organ of self-knowing in terms of the energy field or etheric body is our feeling capacity. And our feeling capacity is an extension of the sense of touch. There are various ways in which we can become aware of this energy field. One way is to have children frequently use Eeman screens.[4]

It should be emphasized at this point that the education of children as well as adults in every stage of life is not a one-shot matter. It is not a matter of listening to a lecture or of reading a book, and then having that be the end of it. The study of even the basic points of this Teaching must be entered into again and again and again, throughout one's life. One must also enter into exercises or forms of activity that relate to the kinds of learning specific to each stage of life.

Thus, the individual in the second stage of life should repeatedly consider this matter of the energy field, or the feeling being. We contact or sense it as energy, but it is manifested through the vehicle of our feeling and emotion. Therefore, individuals in the second stage of life should repeatedly perform exercises in which they can become sensitive to this field.

Using Eeman screens is one effective exercise. Another good method is the exercise that is commonly used to train people in the laying on of hands. This is a practice that children can easily do: Place your hands, open-palmed, directly facing one another. Move the hands

4. Eeman screens, so named after L. E. Eeman, the inventor, are simple metal screens about ten by fifteen inches in size with metal handles. They are used to realign and energize the etheric circuitry (or natural energy field) of the body. See *The Eating Gorilla Comes in Peace*, pp. 412-14, for a more detailed explanation of their use.

back and forth, bringing the palms closer and closer together, but without letting them touch each other. Eventually it feels as if some kind of fluid is being pushed out from underneath your hands, almost as if you were moving them back and forth in water. As you move your hands closer and closer together, this fluid sensation increases and a tingling feeling appears. When this occurs, rotate each hand in a circle, with palms still facing one another. You will feel little filaments of energy coming from each hand being broken or moved around. Children should be asked to do this exercise playfully, and also to play with Eeman screens. In both cases, they should report their sensations and feelings. These and other techniques that you may creatively invent should be used to develop sensitivity to the energy field.

Apart from the growing sensitivity to the energy field, children should develop feeling-sensitivity itself. In other words, children should cultivate the capacity to use the etheric dimension of the being in their contact with everything in the natural world. Using touch and all the other senses, they should develop a feeling sensitivity to the energy and the emotional state of others and to the energies in Nature. Children should also be taught to use all their senses in the physical observation of the material world and other beings. In other words, they should have a feeling-based and not merely a materially based relationship to Nature. However, they must be brought to exercise this feeling dimension on the basis of self-knowledge, having observed their own energy field.

Through the learning process of the second stage of life, including the development of social adaptation and sensitivity to Nature, children should come to realize that their emotional state is registered in their energy field, and that their emotional state communicates itself to others not only through their actions and speech, but also directly, via the interaction of this energy field with the energy field of others. They must learn that one need not even be in proximity to someone to experience the effects of their energy field. The energy field registers states of mind, body, and emotion, as well as psychic states of all kinds, and we involuntarily communicate these states to others. Thus, we affect others and even the natural world via this energy field.

Because this direct communication of our state to others has moral and spiritual implications, we must become responsible for our energy state—responsible, therefore, for our emotional state. We must keep our energy field in balance by transcending reactive emotions, and we must maintain a state of physical well-being and mental openness, receptivity, and clarity. We must maintain a free psychic state. In doing this, we not only change our outward behavior, but we also affect our energy field and therefore our energetic transmission to others.

Thus, in the second stage of life, we learn about this energy field that is the dimension of the personality next in subtlety after the gross physical dimension. The child learns how to be responsible for it, how to communicate through it, and how to be sensitive and helpful to others in these terms. Thus, the child learns how to do massage and laying on of hands, and how to have an altogether healing, enlivening, and quickening effect on others. This kind of learning involves both moral and spiritual training. Thus, moral and spiritual training should be a continuous part of the daily education of children in the second stage of life and even of those transitioning to this stage.

The object is not to merely socialize children in conventional terms, but rather to bring them to the capability to be socialized rationally or in truly human and spiritual terms. Therefore, they should learn how this etheric dimension works and how to use it rightly in all relations from a spiritual and a truly moral point of view.

Let us move on to the third stage:

> Stage 3: The third stage of life involves forms of adaptation that should basically occupy us during the third seven years of life. It is the period of adaptation to the lower astral dimension of the manifest personality. Thus, it involves development of the will, the thinking mind, and the mind of the psyche. The individual should already have developed as a physical, feeling, and moral character, fully in touch with the Living Force of existence. Thus, in the third stage, this personality must develop the will to rightly and fruitfully use the Life-Force in the context of psyche, mind, body, and relations with others in the natural world.
>
> This stage clearly involves development of mental faculties in the form of reasoning power and the capacity to observe and understand self, others, and the world. It also

involves extensive learning in the form of conventional subject matter as well as in the form of a fairly detailed study of the Teaching, the disciplines, and the practices of our Way.

Taking into consideration the level of sophistication of teenagers, "a fairly detailed study of the Teaching" means a basic study of the Teaching and the disciplines. This would entail the study of our practice of diet, exercise, general health principles, service, social life, and those disciplines of meditation that are appropriate at this stage and age. It also includes the study of various other technicalities and the philosophical bases of the conception of the processes of conductivity[5] (or how to be associated with the Life-Current) and real meditation,[6] the structure of the world, and so forth—all from a spiritual point of view. These subjects would be on the curriculum for formal, regular, and continuous study by third stagers, along with the conventional subject matters that must be part of everyone's schooling.

Apart from this, the individual should develop sensitivity to the deeper psyche, or the spontaneous processes of mind that are deeper than ordinary thinking and the social personality. Thus, appropriate meditative exercises of a devotional type should develop in this stage, and the exercise of imagination should, even as earlier in life, be emphasized and rewarded. In addition, the individual should be taught to be sensitive to dreams, even to keep a regular diary that describes nightly dreams and experiences in meditation. And the contents of dreams and meditative experiences should be frequently discussed with adult counselors. In this manner, the individual will develop an

5. "Conductivity" is, in general, the capacity of the body-mind to conduct, or be surrendered into, the All-Pervading Life-Current. Such conductivity or surrender is realized through love, or radiant whole-body feeling to Infinity, and such love involves coordinated engagement of body, breath, and attention in alignment with the Universal Current of Life-Energy.

6. Real meditation, or what Master Da calls the "conscious process," is the senior practice and responsibility of practitioners in each stage of the Way. Founded upon true "hearing" of the Teaching, or release of self into the Transcendental Condition of Divine Ignorance, it is the discipline of conscious surrender of attention in the Divine or Transcendental Being.

awareness and a free acceptance of his or her psychic self, with all of its expansive contents, including the archetypes, subtle or astral phenomena, and possibly even out-of-body experiences, extrasensory perception, premonitory phenomena, and so forth.

The third stage of life is complete when the individual is fully responsible for adult life—not merely in the conventional social sense, or merely because of chronological age, but in the sense that he or she is fully prepared (physically, emotionally, etherically, psychically, mentally, and with a free or intelligent will) to enter into the social, personal, and spiritual responsibilities of true Manhood.

As I have indicated, the individual in the first stage of life is primarily dealing with physical adaptation, or realizing a state of physical individuation and the capacity for social life. In other words, the physical base has primary importance in the first stage. In the second stage of life, physical adaptation of course continues, but the primary base associated with the learning process is the etheric body, the next dimension of our manifest existence. Then, in the third stage of life, the next subtler level of our manifest existence, the lower astral or mental-psychic dimension, is the primary base of education, though obviously the physical and etheric dimensions still remain part of education. Every subsequent stage builds upon the preceding developments. And each stage is associated with a unique new form of study and a new kind of growth.

As was the case in the preceding two stages, in the third stage of life, when the lower astral dimension is to be located and brought into operation, it is not necessarily self-evident or clear to the individual that this next subtler dimension exists. Hopefully, however, the individual brought up in the context of this Way and in our culture will not have received the usual cues given in the world today which suppress our awareness of the etheric and lower astral aspects of our personality, or at least such cues will not have been effective. Prior to the third stage, the individual will have had a continuous life of familiarity with his or her psychic life, without suppressing or discounting dreams or subtle phenomena. However, it is in the third stage in particular that adaptation to the lower astral dimension occurs.

Just as in the previous two stages, what must occur first is education that will familiarize the individual with this lower astral dimension. Various kinds of meditative play will already have occurred in the first and second stages of life—the instructions in *What to Remember to Be Happy* would be part of the meditative education of children from infancy—but in the third stage, the individual should begin to adopt some of the devotional and meditative practices that are taken on by adults in The Free Communion Church.[7] Initially they would practice the Easy Prayer of Surrender.[8] Eventually (probably in the late teens), the practice of the Prayer of Remembrance[9] and the Prayer of Changes[10] may be taken up if a youngster exhibits the appropriate signs. Presumably, these signs will be exhibited as an individual comes of age and thus theoretically approaches the fourth stage of life.

To become familiar with this lower astral dimension, a person in the third stage of life should begin to employ these devotional and meditative practices and also begin to pay special attention to dreams. We can playfully ask children about dreams at an earlier age, but in this stage children should take a rather systematic approach to noticing their dreams. Therefore, I recommend keeping a dream diary. Ideally, dreams should be recorded in the diary each day, shortly after

7. The Free Communion Church is one of four divisions of The Johannine Daist Communion, the spiritual fellowship of practitioners of the Way Taught by Master Da Free John (see p. 126). The Free Communion Church is the educational and cultural organization for maturing practitioners.

8. The Easy Prayer of Surrender is the initial devotional exercise practiced by beginners in the Way of Radical Understanding. Its practice consists of vocal or silent mental invocation of and affirmation of one's surrender to the Radiant Transcendental Being, combined with bodily relaxation into and reception of the Spirit-Current of the Divine.

9. The Prayer of Remembrance is the whole-bodily exercise of invoking and surrendering body and mind into the Divine by means of the Name "Da," which denotes the "Giver" or the Divine Being in its personal aspect. For Master Da's instructions on this practice, see his *Bodily Worship of the Living God,* pp. 141ff.

10. In the practice of the Prayer of Changes, one first exhales and releases all negative or limited conditions of body, mind, and experience, then inhales, receives, and affirms the most positive desired changes in body, mind, and experience while abiding in the disposition of intuitive Communion and tacit identification with the Divine Self, and then changes his or her action in life accordingly. See *Bodily Worship of the Living God,* by Da Free John, pp. 92ff.

waking, when dreams are still fresh and vivid. In other words, children in this stage would develop the habit of being aware of their dreams and remembering them, instead of pressing them out of consciousness into the unconscious when they awaken. Dreams, as well as meditative experiences and any experiences of a subtle, psychic kind, should regularly be discussed with adult counselors. The dream diaries can then also be made available to the counselors, or the children can write periodic summaries of their diaries and submit these prior to counseling. There can also be gatherings in which many children get together with their counselors and discuss their experiences openly.

In the conventional world, the psyche and these lower astral experiences tend to be de-legitimized, just as the energy or etheric dimension of the human personality tends to be de-legitimized. Actually, most people today do not even know that these two dimensions exist, or they doubt their verity, even though they have experiences which indicate the existence of these dimensions. People are conventionally encouraged, even engineered, to presume only a materially based view of reality, and therefore they tend to discount such phenomena and the organs or functional aspects of the being with which these phenomena are associated. Consequently, most people tend never to learn how to function in terms of the etheric and lower astral dimensions of the personality. However, children should be able to enjoy free, open contact with these dimensions, so that they can rightly use this equipment as part of their ordinary humanity. These dimensions should not be suppressed, nor should they be the subject of demonic fascination. Rather, they should be made a matter of responsibility. This means that children must become familiar with the etheric and lower astral dimensions, and we must not fail to help them learn how to relate to them rightly.

All kinds of contents of the lower psyche will be communicated by young people in their diaries and discussions. Many of their dreams will represent ordinary life-stresses, and these should be discussed, and help should be extended to those who obviously have problems. But apart from these ordinary dreams, there are other kinds of significant dreams, such as archetypal dreams and astral experiences (astral dreaming, astral travel, and so forth). Young people may also have out-of-body experiences, various kinds of extrasensory perception, premonitory dreams, or premonitions in the waking state. These represent a real dimension of our personality which we must permit to become active. So, we must notice this subtle, psychic component of the lower astral dimension and become responsible for it. This is the first aspect of learning in the third stage of life.

The whole life of the thinking mind is another component of the lower astral dimension of our being. Individuals in the third stage of life should therefore develop their capacity to reason, to observe and understand. Naturally, they should study in a much more sophisticated fashion than in the previous stages, and cover a wide variety of subjects of a conventional nature as well as material relating to this Way of life.

The third aspect of the lower astral personality is the will. The will is not merely some sort of hard-edged, effortful intention, but rather it should be free intention, based on the openness of the personality. The will is a guide to the Life-Force, and it should gently direct the functions of the lower personality (the lower astral, etheric, and physical dimensions of the being). It embraces what we call psyche, mind, emotion, body, and their whole interplay. The will is the connection between all of those functions and is the medium whereby the Living Force of existence is given form. Therefore, by understanding ourselves in physical, etheric, and astral terms, the will is able to release energy into the whole domain of psyche, mind, emotion, body, and relationships. This kind of learning, or capacity, is the secret of the fulfillment of the third stage of life and of the early career of a human being. The ability of the open, free personality to direct the lower personality by means of the will (or free intention) is basically what makes us human beings.

Thus, at the end of the third stage of life, the young adult should be fully responsible for bringing the Living Force of existence into the domain of the lower personality and its relationships. The individual should be a balanced, socially positive, and spiritually awakened character—a benign personality capable of assuming responsibility in the context of relationships. Such a person should know how to maintain health and how to live a wholesome life. He should also understand a wide variety of things about life, and should have a basic grasp of the spiritual Teaching. The third stage of life, then, is the summary or the crown of the early life of the individual who has achieved competence and responsibility for everything that we ordinarily call human.

The later stages of life lead us into what is beyond the human, what transcends human life and life in Nature. They transform human existence into something more, or more highly evolved than the human. The third stage of life is the stage in which, based on true learning, our Manhood (and this applies to both men and women) is established, and we go on from there to live as true human beings. But we also go on from there to develop our spiritual life, to go beyond human limitations as well as to magnify our human capabilities through the intrusion of the Living Spirit into life.

Now we come to the next stage:

Stage 4: The fourth stage of life, like all the stages that follow, is best conceived without reference to specific chronological age—except that it may generally be said to begin at approximately the age of twenty-one years, or perhaps slightly earlier. It is the stage in which all of the characteristic activities of adulthood begin with full responsibility, but the primary significance of the fourth stage of life, like all stages that follow, is spiritual rather than social or merely functional. The fourth stage of life is the true beginning of the exercise of self-transcendence.

In the fourth stage of life the individual must command all the mechanisms to which he or she has adapted in the first three stages of life. This command should take the form of voluntary alignment and surrender of the physical, etheric, and lower astral dimensions of the manifest personality to the Self-Radiant Transcendental or Divine Condition of Being. This takes the form of an exercise (founded on self-understanding and the life-practice of self-economizing functional and relational disciplines) in which the central or feeling-dimension of the manifest being is made the base for the surrender and transcendence of the physical, etheric, emotional, psychic, and mental personality in the Life-Current, Love-Bliss, and Consciousness of Transcendental Being.

The practice of the fourth stage of life in our Way develops either via the Way of Faith, the Way of Insight, or the first stage of the Perfect Practice,[11] until energy and attention begin to relax from the bondage of the lower personality and more mature spiritual evidence begins to appear.

My discussion of the fourth and following stages will not be as extensive as my discussion of the earlier stages, because so much of our literature is already devoted to the fourth stage and beyond.[12] However, I would like to briefly point out the significance of the fourth stage.

The fourth stage of life is demonstrated traditionally in various kinds of cultural efforts, based on different philosophies. In our Way of life, however, we do not merely practice in the context of the fourth stage of life, but we transcend the dualism that typically characterizes the fourth stage of life in that very process. It is the stage of the true beginning of self-transcendence as a fully responsible exercise in which the lower astral, etheric, and physical dimensions of the personality are surrendered into the Transcendental Condition. The vehicle or base on which this is done is the feeling being. Through the feeling dimension of being, and on the basis of self-understanding, the lower personality is commanded or willed to surrender into the Transcendental Condition.

11. The Way of Faith is the approach to self-transcending practice recommended to the person who is naturally inclined to a devotional disposition or attitude of feeling-surrender.

The Way of Insight is specifically intended for the practitioner who is especially gifted with the capacity to mature by applying his natural discriminative intelligence in the observation, understanding, and transcendence of the self-contraction.

The Perfect Practice is the epitome of the Way of Radical Understanding or Divine Ignorance. It is the foundation of the Way, though few individuals are mature enough to engage it directly, without having to move through the preparatory stages. The Perfect Practice consists of three phases.

In the first phase the discipline is to identify with consciousness in daily life and meditation, until the body-mind accepts the discipline of equanimity. Attention is thus freed for the second phase wherein attention (or self-consciousness itself) is yielded into the Source Condition from which it is always arising. This practice gradually becomes profound Identification with Being or Consciousness Itself. The third phase of the Perfect Practice begins when this Identification becomes complete and the individual simply Abides as Transcendental Divine Consciousness, recognizing all phenomena.

For a complete description of the Perfect Practice, see *The Liberator (Eleutherios)*, by Da Free John.

12. See "The Books of Master Da Free John" at the back of this volume.

This brings us to:

Stage 5: The fifth stage of life follows naturally from the fourth. The same practices that finally developed in the fourth stage are continued, but the experiential evidence that develops in this stage goes beyond the phenomena of the lower coil into the domain of the upper coil,[13] or the domain of cosmic or transpersonal existence. Thus, phenomena associated with higher meditation appear, including higher astral signs, such as experiences of higher subtle worlds, views of the Cosmic Mandala,[14] and even nirvikalpa samadhi.[15] The sixth stage may begin when all of this has been observed and really transcended to the degree that energy and attention are no longer bound to seeking via either the lower or the upper coil of the manifest self. This readiness is shown by the signs of true spiritual maturity, including stable equanimity and the tendency of the Life-Current to magnify Itself in the right side of the heart.[16]

The natural evidence that the fourth stage of life is complete, apart from all the other basic qualifications that pertain to the fourth stage

13. The "lower coil" refers to the gross physical dimension of the body-mind or the complex of functions below the heart, epitomized at the navel. The "upper coil" is the range of higher human functions above the heart, including the subtler dimensions of the psyche.

14. The Cosmic Mandala is a visionary manifestation of the Universal Energy of the Cosmos. It appears as concentric circles of light progressing from red on the perimeter through golden-yellow, silvery-white, dark blue or black, and brilliant blue to the Ultimate White Brightness in the center of the Mandala. In the seventh stage of life, the Conscious being stands beyond the whole cosmic configuration and the mechanics of Nature which it represents. For a full discussion of the Cosmic Mandala, see *Easy Death*, by Da Free John, especially part 4, "Transcending the Cosmic Mandala," pp. 223–88.

15. The Sanskrit term "nirvikalpa samadhi" means literally "formless ecstasy." This elevated mystical experience is aspired to by many traditional yogis. In Master Da Free John's view, however, this state is simply the crowning achievement of yogic practice corresponding to the fifth stage of life. It represents a merely temporary absorption of attention in the Transcendental Consciousness, whereas in the seventh stage of life there is perpetual recognition of all phenomena as non-binding modifications of Radiant Transcendental Being.

16. Master Da Free John has described the area of the heart on the right side of the chest as the center, or root, of the Transcendental Consciousness or Self in the body-mind. This area corresponds to the sinoatrial node (or pacemaker) in the right atrium. For a detailed description of this psycho-physical center and its relationship to Enlightenment, see *The Enlightenment of the Whole Body*, chapter 7.

and all previous stages, is that relaxation of energy and attention from bondage to the lower personality has begun to take place. Then the more mature spiritual evidence of the fifth stage begins to appear. In other words, at some point there will be the natural appearance of upper coil experiences, particularly of that aspect of the upper coil which represents the higher astral dimension of existence. The fourth stage of life is a transitional stage that is basically about developing this capacity for self-transcendence.

On the one hand, the fifth stage, like the first three stages, is a matter of adaptation to a particular functional level of our existence. On the other hand, it is a matter of transcendence of this specific level of existence as well. That dimension of existence to which we adapt and which we transcend in the fifth stage is the higher astral dimension, the higher aspects of the upper coil of the being. The higher astral dimension of our personality reaches beyond personal aspects of the human being (which include the lower astral, etheric, and physical dimensions) into that dimension or domain that we might call transpersonal or cosmic. These signs or experiences of the fifth stage of life naturally and gradually emerge as the fourth stage matures, and through continued practice of the same self-transcending disciplines that are first cultivated in the fourth stage, we transcend our bondage to the possibilities represented by this cosmic or transpersonal aspect of the being.

Even though we transcend the possibilities of the higher astral dimension, we still experience them in meditation and in other moments of waking, dreaming, and sleeping. These experiences may include all the phenomena of higher meditation I have mentioned in this essay—visions of higher subtle worlds, views of the Cosmic Mandala, unusual lights and sounds, and so forth. Even nirvikalpa samadhi may appear. However, the fifth stage of life has completed itself not when one or more of these experiences have occurred, but when the signs are present that the individual is no longer bound to the purposes of either the lower or upper coil, and that he is not seeking these phenomena for their own sake, but is rather in a state of natural equanimity in which energy and attention are free of the binding efforts associated with the lower and upper coils. In other words, nirvikalpa samadhi is not a necessary precondition for entrance into the sixth stage. Obviously, some forms of subtle phenomena will have occurred if real meditation is active, but the qualifications for the sixth stage of life are simply those just described as spiritual maturity in the fifth stage of life.

Another sign that may also appear in the fulfillment phase of the fifth stage of life is evidence that the Life-Current is magnifying Itself in the right side of the heart, rather than in the brain core, or in the crown of the head, or in some other bodily center.

Next I would like to characterize the sixth stage of life:

> Stage 6: In our Way, the sixth stage of life is encountered and transcended via the second stage of the Perfect Practice. I will not discuss this or the seventh stage at length here since it is all fully elaborated in the existing literature. Suffice it to say that this stage is complete when the Transcendental Self, the Root-Source of attention and all phenomenal conditions, is fully Realized and the "eyes open," or tacit recognition of self, others, and world is firm and true.

Now we come to the ultimate stage:

> Stage 7: In this, the fully Enlightened stage of life, there is simply Self-Abiding recognition of phenomenal existence as a transparent, or merely apparent, unnecessary, and nonbinding modification of Self-Radiant Transcendental Being. This Process shows the evidence of Transfiguration, Transformation, and Indifference, until Perfect Translation[17] from conditional phenomenal existence and into the Transcendental Domain of Being.

---

17. "Transfiguration," "Transformation," and "Translation" are technical terms that describe the unfolding process of God-Realization in the seventh stage of life. Transfiguration is the pervasion of body and mind by Transcendental Radiance or Light. Bodily and mental Transformation involves the arising of supernormal signs or abilities, such as healing power, longevity, and psychic capabilities. Divine Translation is the ultimate evidence of God-Realization, wherein the limited psycho-physical body, mind, and world are no longer noticed-- not because the consciousness has withdrawn from all such phenomena, but because it has entered into such profound absorptive Realization of the Divine Condition that all phenomena are, as Master Da says, "Outshined" by that Light.

That completes the essay. As you will appreciate, it is a summary of the education or the way of schooling associated with the seven stages of life in this Way. It pays particularly detailed attention to the first three or perhaps four stages of life, although there are some details specified for the fifth stage as well. Obviously then, this essay concentrates on the aspects of education in the earlier stages of life that make it possible for people to transition into the spiritual practice of life. The later stages are more elaborately described in our basic literature.

Does anyone have any questions, or is there some aspect on which I should further elaborate?

DEVOTEE: Could you say something more about assuming responsibility for one's sexuality in the third stage of life?

MASTER DA FREE JOHN: Well, I mentioned in the description of the second stage of life that the schooling in that stage is not directly sexual, although it should provide the living emotional base for later sexual activity. I also stated that genital sexuality and social patterns of a demonstrably sexual nature should be conserved or by-passed through right understanding until the third stage of life is complete, so that we may first develop full human responsibility for what must become the yoga of sexual communion. Thus, individuals in the third stage of life should not have to deal with all the problems and concerns associated with an active sexual life.

Among the things that third stagers should study, however, is the whole matter of sexuality and sexual reproduction. They should particularly study the practical matters associated with sex when they get a little older, but they do not have to be too far into their teens to begin some basic study of sexuality. In any case, from very early childhood, our children should be helped to understand their sexual interest.

In this Way of life, sexuality is not taboo, and it is not to be suppressed. The message to be communicated to children or to young people is not that it is ideally better not to be sexual. Rather, what should be communicated to them is an understanding of sexuality that is spiritually based, and we want to help them to prepare for sexuality in that form. We want to guide them to rightly by-pass overt sexual activity until they are fully prepared for sexual practice in the form of a spiritual yoga.

Sexual activity should begin after the third stage of life, and no earlier than the very late teen years, if it is to be founded on full maturity in the first three stages of life as they are described in the essay. When young people become sexually active, they must at first learn about and adapt to sex itself, but they should do this based on their fully developed character as someone who was properly guided through the first three stages of life. As fourth stagers, they should be helped within the context of our community to develop their sexual activity as the yoga of sexual communion, and not merely to indulge sex as a conventional means of relieving stress or merely as a reproductive act. What should be communicated to our children is how to be sexual, not how to avoid sexuality or suppress it, but they should also understand its proper development in the first three stages of life.

In these first three stages, children will experience certain kinds of sexual feelings, and they will develop different kinds of sexual character—girls learn how to be girls, and boys how to be boys. There are also various kinds of play which are associated with sexual role modeling. Adults simply have to stay in real time with children and young people, and have a fully open, communicative relationship with them, so that when any evidence of sexual activity appears, one can be instructive in terms of their present moment of interest or involvement with it.

For the first seven years of life, sexual activity is rarely a significant feature of children's lives. Parents should not slap their wrists or threaten and yell at them for sexual play and mutual exploration. They should perhaps find some artful way to divert them, as we do not want them to become obsessed with sexual play, but basically children should just be allowed to explore this matter, feel into it, and play with it. There is nothing very important about it, as they are not really in a position to understand much about sexuality in the first seven years, particularly the first four or five years. It is only after the age of five or six, when they start to develop perhaps a little more interest in it and move out socially more, that you can begin to discuss sexuality with them. Then you can introduce them to the whole matter of feeling-sensitivity, right social life, and the right enjoyment of life in general.

Adults should help them to understand and not merely suppress their interest in sexuality. They should help them understand what it may have to do with reproduction, and what it may have to do with their life later on. Diverting them from any fascination with it in a very natural, artful way helps them to simply feel this energy whole bodily, and develop an expanded emotional and feeling life, an energetic life, without indulging this bodily based, self-based interest. Because if they indulge it, they will become Narcissistic and sexually retarded, and it will be very difficult for them to develop a yogic sexual life later on.

Adults need to advance young people's understanding of sexuality, particularly as they enter their teens. As they enter their teens or pass into puberty, their sexual interest is likely to become intensified because of the hormonal changes that are occurring in the body. We need to assist them at that point by explaining to them that these hormonal changes are for the purpose of growth, preparing their bodies for adult life. Even though sexual feelings may be associated with the glandular stimulation accompanying this growth, they should not be indulged. Young people should simply understand what it is they are passing through and release their concentration on these feelings. They should open and devote themselves to the larger learning and discipline of the brahmacharya[18] stage of life.

Thus, during the third stage of life, parents should help young people to by-pass overt sexual interest through reasonable, artful techniques.

The point to be emphasized is that we should not suppress our children's sexual interest. No one should horrify or threaten them, or create sex-negative views in them. Rather, they should be educated to a sex-positive view or a view that ultimately can become freely sexual, if they will choose it. They should be able to devote the first three stages of life to the development of the whole human personality on a spiritual base, and the by-passing of sexual indulgence is a form of learning that strengthens them, and permits the process of full human growth to

18. "Brahmacharya" (or *brahmacarya*) is a Sanskrit word meaning literally "conduct in consonance with the Absolute." In the Hindu spiritual traditions, it has widely been equated with the lifelong practice of intentional or motivated celibacy by spiritual aspirants. But this Sanskrit term originally referred to the student stage of life, generally conceived to occupy the first twenty-five years of life. During those years, the growing individual (or brahmacharin) was formally trained in the Way and Truth of existence. This period generally involved strict celibacy until marriage, or entrance into the householder's stage of life. Over time, the term "brahmacharya" has become synonymous with celibacy itself, even though the ancient practice of brahmacharya encompassed all of the common areas of life, including academic studies, music, art, diet, work, the Scriptures, and so forth.

occur. It keeps them from becoming aberrated through sexual stimulation.

Without the understanding of the first three stages of life, sexual self-indulgence is just as aberrating as sexual repression. Neither should rightly be part of the life of children and young people. You all know from having lived in a rather chaotic fashion, without a real program of cultural and human adaptation and growth, how you have suffered in your sexuality as a child, a teenager, and an adult. You know how much of an impediment this arbitrary and false sexual learning has been to your later life and to your spiritual life. The conception of sexual education that I am communicating to you should help people to avoid the difficulty of that dilemma. It is a simple matter of right learning and artful communication. If it is approached in this fashion, and all the kinds of learning I have described here are developed, then those who grow up in this community and come into their late teens and early twenties should be stable, balanced, and spiritually awake people, with full human capability, who can naturally practice sexual communion, as well as all the other forms of practice in this Way of life. In other words, they should not have to go through any neurotic sexual episodes.

Obviously, the success of this approach depends on counseling, on good relations between children and adults, and it requires sensitivity on the part of the adults to the situation of our children and youngsters. They will have some difficulties, but the difficulties should not be taken seriously. Adults should simply provide them a way out of their difficulties, and this way is the positive spiritual and human process altogether. That is the secret. In every case, draw them into the spiritual process. Do not let them become involved in all kinds of deep, heavy, obsessive considerations of their sexual and other problems. All such problems arise only because children or young people have been diverted from the process of life, as it presents itself in terms of the first three stages. If they are led back into that process, any problem will naturally fall away, and a state of balance will be achieved. Thus, rather than keying in on problems, one should notice and discuss them, and draw their attention into the right process of living.

Nothing is denied to teenagers by their not being sexually active. On the contrary, they will be greatly helped if they can retain the Living Force and avoid self-possessed involvement in sex until they have fully developed as human beings, with all the capabilities I have described here. Then they can choose to be sexually active and create whatever pattern they will, based on a balanced and strong life background. They will be able to practice sexuality freely rather than neurotically, as all of you did and are doing even now. Instead of moving into the process of sexual communion, all of you are spending years working out sex-based emotional neuroses!

Where did you get all of those neuroses? You created them by one or another kind of failure in each of the first three stages of life. You are still childish, or rather, infantile; you have not fully individuated physically; you still tend to lapse into dependency modes in which you, in effect, want to meld with your mother again. You have great difficulty achieving a state of self-responsible, physical individuation and balance, because of some emotional impediment associated with your childhood or infancy. You suffer sexual aberrations, emotional problems, and reactive tendencies which dominate your lives. The primary reason for this, apart from all the kinds of negative adaptation and unfortunate life circumstances, is that you did not achieve a state of direct sensitivity to your etheric life, your energy life, and how that affects other people. You never developed a sense of yourself as being greater than the physical, and you never exercised yourself as energy, as a spirit. You never became responsible for the energy mechanism that is primarily an emotional mechanism. Thus, you tend to be reactive rather than clear, balanced, and free.

The etheric dimension, you see, is controlled by emotion and sex. Sex is the physical expression or counterpart of emotion. To become obsessively self-involved with sex, therefore, is to collapse the etheric dimension of the personality, and to eliminate the emotional force and therefore the Life-Force from the sex act. Instead of being an emotionally free expression of the living being, the sex act becomes merely a means for discharging the body of its life-feeling. When there is a lot of Life-Energy in the body and you are emotionally or otherwise contracted, then you feel uptight. The body is like a circuit or a hose conducting the Life-Current. If you have a knot in it, you get uptight. The more water there is in the pipe or the more energy there is in the circuit, the more intense the pain. And you use sex to rid yourself of this pain. Instead of removing the contraction, you displace the energy, leaving the contraction in place.

Thus, if you do not have the virtues of true growth in the third stage of life, you cannot practice right sex. It just cannot be done. This is the reason why merely functional sexual activity should not occur in the third stage of life. The virtues of celibacy in this stage should be rightly understood as not merely the prevention of sex, but as the releasing of all tension associated with sexual interest. This is done so that one can learn to live a spiritual or whole life, maintain a balance of energy and a free psyche, and develop the whole personality in spiritual terms in preparation for, among other things, right sexual activity. Thus, it is the fulfillment of the process of the third stage of life, based on the fulfillment of the processes in the second and first stages, that makes right sexual activity possible. Therefore, sexual activity is basically to be by-passed, although learned about and prepared for, until the fourth stage of life. To me, sexual sanity basically depends on the effective occurrence of this process.

Are there any other questions?

DEVOTEE: Master, I would like to know how to use the dreams of children in the second stage of life. I have noticed that the content of most of their dreams is more emotional than of the nature of the psychic or astral phenomena you just described. They want to relate their dreams and talk about them a lot, and I do not know how to consider their dreams with them most effectively.

MASTER DA FREE JOHN: In all stages of life, including the first, children, and then later young people, should have an open, communicative counseling relationship with one or more adults. This should not merely be a formal, abstract relationship, but a friendship, a right relationship with one or more adults. We should be talking to children about their dreams and any other kinds of unusual experiences not only in the second stage but in the first and third stages as well. We should be rather imaginative in our discussions with them and artfully question them even from earliest life, not merely to find out whether or not they are having any unusual experiences, but also to let them know that it is alright to have such experiences. If they have such experiences, we should let them know that it is right and good to talk about them with adults with whom they are intimate.

The question you are asking really relates not just to the second stage, but to the first and all other stages as well. As the first principle, one should have a good, communicative relationship that is not suppressive and that does not suggest to children that there are only certain kinds of experiences which are acceptable. You said, for instance, that second stagers tend primarily to communicate dreams with an emotional content, or a content perhaps suggesting emotional conflicts in daily life. The fact that they are having dreams only of this kind, or at least are only reporting dreams of this kind, could have much to do with what has been suggested to them throughout their lives. They may somehow have the impression that this is the only kind of dream they should have or talk about. Perhaps their learning altogether has not been rightly supervised, so that they have basically been led to become concentrated in emotionally aberrated, self-concerned states, and not to be more open and expansive in their expression.

Adults should, of course, discuss dreams with children, no matter what their content. They should not sit and analyze them like a psychiatrist, but rather should simply get children to be communicative about their dreams, listen to what they tell us about their problems, and then deal with those problems in practical and appropriate ways. It is our responsibility to draw them away from any concern with problems or aberrations and into the principles of real practice, into social relationship wherein these aberrations will be balanced out and released. This is always the essence of the right approach.

In addition to discussing whatever dreams our children may want to relate to us, or tend to have, we should help them to have better and more interesting dreams. The book *What to Remember to Be Happy* is rather aphoristic and is intended to suggest something to children, but also something to the adults who are educating them. It suggests to the children that they are more than what they look like, and it also suggests a way of exploring the other dimensions of their existence. In other words, it suggests an approach to educating children that helps them to be sensitive to what they are that is more than their physical existence. Therefore, children can become more profoundly involved with the meditation exercises in *What to Remember to Be Happy* which will help to change the quality of their dreams and other experiences. So, in accordance with my instructions in *What to Remember to Be Happy*, children should spend a reasonable amount of time in meditation, and truly relax beforehand. They should sometimes meditate alone, not in the room with other children, and they should meditate more seriously.

We should not suggest to children that there are only certain things that may occur during meditation, so that they just prattle back to us images that have been suggested to them. If this meditative exercise is ever going to show any evidence of higher psychic activity or be reflective of the deep psyche in the lower astral dimension, children must learn to relax deeply. Likewise, if dream phenomena are ever to have a higher quality, children must be able to rest deeply, and be free of stress and emotional conflict before going to bed. In other words, they must be in an essentially healthy state, sensitive to their feeling life and their connectedness to existence through the energy vehicle.

This connection, you see, replaces the mother-child connection, and the mother-child connection is an unconscious one in which the child does not experience himself or herself separately, or as an individual separate from the mother. Spiritual Communion, Communion with the Living Force, is based on individuation, on your knowing that you are there participating in and surrendering into It. When children are instructed in the right practice of the exercises in *What to Remember to Be Happy*, the quality of their dreams will change and more unusual phenomena will occur in their meditation.

For younger children in the first two stages of life, all this should be communicated as a kind of play, a free kind of Happy activity, but one that requires relaxation, and so forth. Therefore, among the things we want to help them realize is a way to be relaxed and balanced, and not just stressfully vital. If they are stressfully vital, they will tend to have emotional and social problems, be reactive, and have bad dreams and no meditation. The same is true of adults. You must be capable of relaxation and balance, contact with the Living Force and with the psyche, in order for meditation to be fruitful and significant.

We should always expand, rather than limit, the possibilities of children. Sometimes, the questions they are asked seem to elicit only a reaction from them. In other words, their response tends to be limited, for whatever reason, by our suggestions or by their tendencies. Therefore, we should ask the questions differently, introduce the possibility of being more expanded and imaginative—but not merely imaginative, as we also do not want them to create meditative experiences and dreams. Rather, they should be free to <u>allow</u> the psyche to show its signs. One of the ways whereby we ourselves become free to do that is to expand our own capacity, and that means we must become a little more imaginative. Ask children different kinds of questions, ask yourself different kinds of questions, give yourself more possibilities! Do whatever you have to do to break out of your rigid program, and do everything you can to keep children from becoming rigidly programmed. If you have children that already show the signs of such programming, then you must help them break out of it, to become more at ease, more balanced, open, and sensitive.

Clearly, one of the major aspects in the development of children is socialization. It tends to be the purpose of life in common society, whereas from our point of view, it is simply part of the evidence of rightly developing human life. Our children are taught how to cooperate, how to relate to one another in a feeling way, and so forth, but they must learn to do all of that on the basis of our practice. Therefore, in keeping with their age and level of sophistication, they should always be practicing some form of self-understanding and therefore self-release or self-transcendence. Even from a very early age, they should all be practicing some form of spiritual exercise, some way of getting in touch with energy and psyche and what is beyond self.

I have communicated forms of spiritual exercise appropriate for every stage of life. *What to Remember to Be Happy* is a basic guide for the first two stages. Then, in the third stage, devotional and conductivity exercises and rudimentary meditation are introduced, first in the form of the Easy Prayer, and then later on, in the mid-teens or so, when the young person is prepared, in the form of the Prayer of Remembrance and the Prayer of Changes.

If you consider all these elements of practice, you can see that each day in the life of a third stager would be very full, and that is as it should be. It would be a program of life that is very full and very interesting. It would include everything from meditation in the morning, keeping a diary, exercising, and group discussions, to all the different kinds of study, perhaps even computer learning, speed-reading, study of the Teaching, detailed study of all our disciplines, considerations about sexuality and the purposes of the brahmacharya stage, devotional gatherings, and sacramental occasions. There is no end to the possibilities. Each day's program should also include time for socializing. Serving together is, in fact, a form of socializing. Serving together should be fun, should have a human quality to it, and not just be a form of rote discipline that everyone resists. There should also be time for sports and play, but it should all be done in the context of real practice based on moment to moment self-understanding, self-transcendence, and spiritual exercise. Participation in everything should be from that point of view.

All these activities need to be rightly guided by adults, and young people should know they are not the equivalent of little adults. They are not children any more, but neither are they adults. They are individuated physical, emotional, and social personalities in the third stage of life. They should not live like the children of parents, but rather should live as third stage individuals responsible to the adult community that is there to maintain and counsel their daily culture of practice and to instruct them and help them pass through the period of learning that is specific to the third stage of life. Then, when they leave the brahmacharya school in their late teens or so, they would live in the larger community and assume not just the adult responsibilities of work and sex and so forth, but all the forms of our adult spiritual exercises. That is what we should be preparing them for, and not just keeping them in some kind of a "boarding school" until they come of legal age and can run out into the world and blow their minds. That whole urge, in fact, should be transcended in them if they really participate in the culture of this Way in the brahmacharya school.

All of our life, then, is a school, with seven different stages. Whatever our age, we are always going to school, and there is a specific school for each age or time of life, depending on our previous preparation. The third stage of life is not the end of school. It is the end of one school and a passage to another. It is the time of preparation for living an adult life without having to be a lunatic, without having to be an ordinary, worldly person. Thus, having gone through that process, young people should value and appreciate all the things associated with a true spiritual community. Then they would not be thinking about leaving the community. Rather, they would have learned to value it because of its uniqueness in comparison with the rest of the world. They should be capable of functioning in the world while living in our community, but they should fully value what it means to be able to live in such a community and be free of the destiny of a merely aberrated life.

Are there any other questions?

DEVOTEE: I have been considering your description of the first stage of life, in which children develop awareness of their physical individuation. Could you elaborate on the art of developing that awareness without closing off their sensitivity to what they feel even as an infant, prior to becoming a physically individuated being?

MASTER DA FREE JOHN: Well, there should not be any tendency to close them off from anything. It simply should be understood that a basic principle of the first stage of life is that a child becomes organized around a physically individuated existence. But you should not otherwise suppress anything psychically, mentally, or emotionally. Children in the first stage will not demonstrate much sophistication in these terms, but all of their emotional, mental, and psychic experience should simply be allowed to be whatever it is, and you should ask them about it or let them be communicative about it.

Children, you see, are not merely physical individuals. They have all the other dimensions as well. It is just that as the stages of life progress, we learn to be responsible for those dimensions, whereas at an earlier stage, we are less responsible and perhaps to some degree less sensitive to those dimensions.

DEVOTEE: Can a young child's inability to communicate about a particular dimension affect his or her awareness of it?

MASTER DA FREE JOHN: Some children naturally have a kind of psychic life and a highly developed etheric life, and they will show you the evidence of that if you do not suppress it. Others simply do not have it. It may develop later on, but it is just not particularly evident at the time. However, the etheric and astral dimensions of the personality do exist for everyone, and young children in the first stage should of course be drawn into a feeling life and sensitivity to others.

After the age of two or so, they should be allowed and encouraged to discuss dreams, play imaginative games, and playfully do the practices described in *What to Remember to Be Happy*. Whatever evidence there is of the development of their etheric and psychic life, they should be encouraged to communicate about it. If there is no evidence, they should not be made to feel that there is something wrong with them. It may develop later on as they begin to achieve a more conscious involvement with these dimensions.

Most people may not have much significant experience of a higher or a lower astral kind, even of an etheric kind, until they are educated relative to those dimensions. People must be brought concretely into conjunction with these dimensions, and brought to observe them and participate in appropriate spiritual exercises to the point that energies begin to be released in these dimensions. Then the evidence of these dimensions, which was previously unconscious or never even developed as experience, will begin to appear.

We want to make it possible for the living energy in individuals to be fully present in every dimension of their being and thus to ultimately permit them to transcend phenomenal entanglement. The problem with conventional learning is that the Life-Force tends to get limited primarily to the physical dimension and our emotional reaction to that, and our exercise of mind is merely the activity of thinking. We want to make it possible for people not only to use their energies in those terms, but to allow their energies to expand, to be fully present in the etheric dimension so that their aura is strong and full of life pleasure, and so that their psyche will flower. We want to help people to know about themselves beyond the stark waking personality and the social personality. We want them to know about themselves and fully, legitimately exist in terms that go beyond the social personality. Thus, people should have a full psychic existence, even though ultimately, psychic contents must be transcended or released into a pure radiance of the being. In the course of development, however, just as much energy should be going into the free psyche as into thinking, so that just as much energy is going into free feeling as is going into at least the potential for ordinary emotional activity. If that occurs, then the whole program of emotional reactivity will begin to break up, and the individual will become more and more characterized by free feeling rather than by negative, reactive emotions.

We want the Life-Force to be fully available in the body—made available through a science of functional life which teaches the individual how to treat the body, how to exercise, eat, be sexual, and so on. His or her physical existence would be a Transfigured expression of the Living Reality and not just an aberrated, confined, Narcissistic existence limited primarily to the physical base, the thinking mind, and reactive emotion.

Unfortunately, most people are just the physical body, reactive emotion, and the thinking mind. Very little else enters into the context of their existence. They do not know That which transcends self and Nature, That which is the true Divine. They do not even know the subtler aspects of their own phenomenal existence. They are not familiar with the etheric or astral dimensions or with the psyche. They are not alive in free terms. They are confined beings, self-possessed, Narcissistic egos, not in touch with their expanded or subtler self, and not in touch with That which transcends self and Nature. And that is why people are as they are, and the world is as it is. It is the way it is not because we are inherently bound or living in a hell, but because we are not Enlightened. And even that would not be an impediment if we had the service of Enlightened beings, and people lived in a culture of progressive training in true and higher human terms, and also in ultimate terms. Bereft of such service and culture, however, people are limited to the usual egoic and reactive life. And they are aberrated and un-Happy.

Therefore, we must become educated in truly human terms. Even from conception there are responsibilities of mothers that directly affect every aspect of the child—physically, emotionally, mentally, psychically, and spiritually. Thus, we want to educate everyone from conception on to live in freedom, to live in Truth, and to adapt rightly, stage by stage, to every function of their being and to the Ultimate Condition. That is what this description is all about, then. It is an unconventional school of learning, but it is the right convention for learning. In other words, if we understand life and have truly observed it and entered into it and are living it in Truth, we know that this unconventional school of learning is the right process, and we know therefore how we should live with and educate children, young people, and everyone else.

We already know what the result is when we do not do what we should do and when they do not do what they should do. It is the usual ego, the troubled person who causes unlimited problems for himself and others. As egos, we not only create problems for one another by what we are doing and communicating both verbally and emotionally in outward physical terms, but we also transmit it throughout the universe, like super-powered transmitter stations, particularly directing it to those individuals, groups, places, and processes on which our attention is fixed. We are always broadcasting our states to one another, and we even bring about changes in Nature through our individual and collective habits at the level of energy, in the subtler dimension of personality and in the psyche. Thus, if our individual lives and our relationships are meant to change and if human life is going to change altogether, we must become responsible for these habits. If we do not, then we will continue to physically act in ways by which we trouble and aberrate one another, and we will also directly broadcast our aberration to one another through the medium of our energy and psychic dimensions.

All of us are continually receiving these aberrated messages, and if we are not responsible for ourselves, we are affected by them in various ways. We involuntarily move into states of contraction, reactivity, loss of well-being, mental obsession, and all the rest of it. Very often these actions have nothing whatever to do with anything that is going on directly in our lives. They simply come over us, because of the mechanical clicking of our reactive Narcissism and its automaticities, but also through the reception of tendencies in the field of energy. We receive these tendencies from people to whom we are related, and from all kinds of gross and subtle entities, both incarnate and discarnate. These other persons or entities may not have a particular intention relative to us, but they are in a certain state, and for some reason or other, we become subject to them, come into contact with them, experience their influence, and then we ourselves start undergoing changes. But, no matter what changes we tend to go through by these means, we must become responsible for them. This means we must be spiritually awake and practice self-understanding, self-transcendence, and spiritual exercise, and on that basis engage life. Then we will always be repairing and balancing out our auras and our psyches, no matter what effects are tending to impinge on us. We will not become the persona who is characterized by these reactions, by these signs. We should always be able to purify our state and rebalance ourselves, no matter what the circumstance.

Among the things you must learn is how to identify what has to do with you and what has to do with someone else. You do not have to work out every apparent problem. A lot of the time you simply must realize that it is someone else's problem, someone else's state! You do not have to investigate it at all. All you have to do is take a couple of breaths and surrender. Let it go.

There are also things that are part of your own mechanics and part of some of your relationships with which you need to deal. But this wisdom, this Teaching, and this process of life give you all the arms that a human being needs for dealing with this manifest condition of existence, for growing in the midst of it regardless of the circumstances, and for ultimately transcending it. It is up to you to practice or not, and you will tend not to practice if you are weak and unlearned. Therefore, you must learn and become strong first. Then, by practice, you will grow in wisdom and strength. That is what is said about Jesus, is it not? First he had to learn and become strong, and then he grew in Wisdom and stature. First understand yourself and become strong with the Living Presence, the Living Baptism. Then practice. And, if you practice that which you have learned or realized, and That which you have received or entered into, It will magnify Itself in your own person and in all your relationships.

PART II

INTIMACY, DISCIPLINE, AND ECSTASY

INTRODUCTION TO PART II

As was pointed out in the introduction to part 1, the education "system" initiated by Master Da Free John increases the growing individual's experiential horizon. In the opening chapter of this part, it is shown that this process must go hand in hand with a constant expansion of the person's sphere of intimacy. In George P. Elliott's definition, intimacy is "that outreaching in mutuality which, when it is not sentimentalized or perverted, informs the deepening consciousness."[1] It is the kind of open, vulnerable sharing of oneself with another being which barely exists in our ill-at-ease civilization. Intimacy is a trusting, human gesture that makes people emotionally available to each other, beyond the formalities of conventional role-playing. It puts them in touch with the feeling-reality of their lives, and thus creates a basis for personal growth. As the title of the first talk suggests, intimacy is the healing principle—the principle that makes hale or whole, that supports growth rather than fragmentation and dissociation.

Conventional schooling, embedded as it is in the technological-scientistic ideology of the day, actively undermines the possibility of intimacy and instead compounds the anxious self-encapsulation and anonymity which mark and cripple the lives of most of our contemporaries. Children are mass-processed to become conforming, pliable members of what Elliott styled the "pseudoculture" of our consumer society. Even in so-called progressive schools, where the distinction between children and adult teachers is deliberately de-emphasized in order to allow children full freedom of expression, real intimacy is not recognized as a sound principle of human interaction and learning in particular.

One of the great obstacles to intimacy is the schizoid attitude that is cultivated in children about their sexuality. The educational establishment and conservative parents deal with the "sex problem" largely by ignoring it, with perhaps some clumsy gestures toward

1. G. P. Elliott, "The Enemies of Intimacy," *The Laughing Man,* vol. 3, no. 1 (1982), p. 28.

formal—that is, purely biological—sex instruction, in which the emotional component of sex is studiously avoided. Children still obtain sex information—not always quite reliable, and sometimes outrageously incorrect—from other children and from doubtful sources such as the mass media.

Progressive schools tend to be more sex-positive, but all too often this takes the form of inappropriate leniency with children in the midst of their natural inclination toward self-indulgence. But how can teachers give moral guidance when sexuality is not viewed within a framework that extends beyond mere morality to include the supreme value of self-transcendence, or God-Realization? It is one thing not to create sexual guilt in children, and another to connive at their characteristically abandoned expression of their vital nature which, sooner or later, involves sexual activity. In his talk "Surrender of the Body in God," Master Da Free John outlines an approach that is sex-positive but not imprudently tolerant. He explains how the typical sexual problems faced by adolescents can be avoided by channelling the child's natural delight at self-exploration properly: The child should be made to understand, and experience, that Happiness is prior to pleasure and that pleasure, while being perfectly legitimate, is not synonymous with genital pleasure. This lesson, he argues, can be learned by the child if he or she is taught early on to live in relationship rather than as a self-contained unit, a replica of Narcissus.[2]

Liberal approaches decry discipline. Yet, discipline—whether as an imposed standard or as self-discipline—is part of mature social existence. To simply remove the coercive element of conventional education, as is done in most "free-learning" schools such as the Summerhill-type institutions, without introducing new motivations, leaves the child dangling and merely reinforces the sense of egoic independence. However, in the context of spiritual practice and a more broadly conceived destiny for Man, education must fully acknowledge the associative or relational nature of existence. As Master Da Free John emphasized throughout his Teaching work,

2. Narcissus, the self-lover of Greek mythology, is a key symbol in Master Da Free John's description of Man as a self-possessed seeker, one who suffers in dilemma, contracted upon himself at every level of the being from all relations and from the condition of relationship itself.

relationship is the essence of existence. It is Reality itself. And the avoidance of relationship is the perpetual failure of the ego-bound individual. Intimacy is an expression, on the level of social interaction, of that universal relationship. As such it is an antidote to the "usual man's" avoidance of relationship. It is also the foundation for discipline, or the demand to be relational.

A major aspect of such discipline is the cultivation of equanimity, as is explained in the next chapter, entitled "Sila: The Discipline of Equanimity." Equanimity optimizes the available energy and attention, freeing them up for the process of maturation and spiritual transformation.

When the body-mind is out of balance, energy and attention are necessarily drawn into the body-mind complex. Only in a state of complete balance or resonance are energy and attention naturally at rest in their Source. In a state of balance or equanimity we are naturally able to be Occupied with the Divine.[3]

Discipline is a matter for both children and adults. In fact, it is only when the educators and the adult community at large are seen to adopt a life of discipline that the children can become naturally adapted to discipline as well. However, a community in which self-transcending discipline is treasured, but which is not repressive, is slow to be created. For, it rests as much on individual as on communal effort. And old habit patterns are not easily broken. Hence Master Da Free John's persistent but compassionate criticism of the culture of adults and the culture of children in the community of practitioners as well as the larger secular culture. Chapters 5 and 6 demonstrate his unflagging, fiery demand for the intensification of everyone's spiritual commitment and practice, and the right relationship to the Teaching and the Teacher.

3. Da Free John, *"I" Is the Body of Life*, p. 104.

Chapter 2

Intimacy Is the Healing Principle

based on a talk by Da Free John[1]
July 19, 1980

The purpose of discipline is to provide children with conditions through which they may adapt to the laws of life, or the demand for a relational and sacrificial disposition. The key to helping children make this adaptation is to integrate them into social conditions and behavior to the point of enjoyment—in other words, to draw them into a sphere of intimacy. Once a child has learned to enjoy relational life, or the circumstance of intimacy, then the basic discipline for improper behavior is to temporarily withdraw the privilege of social contact, though without bodily punishment.

The effectiveness of such discipline, however, rests entirely on a free and Happy approach to the child. Obviously, not everyone is able to practice this discipline, because it requires a profoundly loving commitment to the child. Therefore, parents, teachers, and other adult intimates must awaken to this responsibility so that it becomes possible to truly serve the child through this approach. Strong, dependable, and loving relationships with children form the foundation for the application of discipline, through which children are aided in their adaptation to a lawful way of life. When this discipline of temporary separation or exclusion is practiced without the background of an intimate love relationship, it becomes a very dehumanizing and non-sympathetic approach, and the child is likely to become more and

1. This chapter is derived from a talk by Master Da Free John, except for the example given by the teacher from Big Wisdom Free School. Founded in 1978, the Big Wisdom Free School system comprises several schools in the United States and abroad, including The Garden of Lions, an ashram school situated outside Hunter, New York.

more exaggerated in the very qualities that the discipline was intended to address.

So long as intimacy is firmly established, temporary separation from the social circumstance is useful, because it allows the child to recognize what he or she truly values, and what is truly of value, which is love and intimacy. Such discipline puts the child in a position in which he or she can and must make choices based on what is valuable: The child can react and dramatize, or he or she can choose to be in relationship in a circumstance of love and intimacy.

It is not easy for a child to recognize what is valuable in the midst of the bombardment of experience that anyone encounters during childhood. If we are to help children to realize that intimacy is the primary value, then love must prevail in the child's life. Only in this way can intimacy be brought into the foreground of his or her experience. If the pleasure of intimacy is absent, if love is not freely given, then the child is automatically reduced to manipulative, reactive efforts to attain love and attention.

Based on this consideration, there are three principles that must be strictly adhered to when a child is dramatizing and requires discipline:

1. Do not assume a problem. Rather, assume a happy willingness to serve the child, based on your understanding that the child's unhappiness is an opportunity for him or her to hear the Teaching and for you to serve the child in that hearing.[2]

2. Ask the child to talk about how he or she feels. All children, and preschoolers in particular, tend to regress to a nonverbal state when suppressing emotions. It is important to draw them into a relational disposition in which humor and sympathy for the ordinary man's dilemma can be expressed on both your parts.

3. Be creative in bringing the child an alternative to his or her unhappy action.

Basically, there is one thing that children are reacting to, and that is the absence of intimacy. Reactive emotions and inappropriate behavior in general are secondary symptoms of a primary frustration.

2. "Hearing" is a technical expression used by Master Da Free John to describe the intuitive understanding of the self-contraction and simultaneous intuitive awakening to Transcendental Consciousness that arise through disciplined study of the argument of the Adept. Such hearing is the foundation for the practice of true spiritual life.

What is being frustrated is intimacy, or life-positive, associative energy. Thus, you cannot deal with these secondary, reactive emotions directly, as if they were the point. What the child is actually suffering is the point, and that is what must be addressed in him or her. A circumstance must be provided in which the primary emotion of love can be expressed or chosen in any moment.

One of the teachers at Big Wisdom Free School furnished an account of a second-stage girl which illustrates this principle of necessary prior intimacy. In class, this child showed little attention, and although she was of above-average intelligence and ability, her studies were difficult for her and minimally fruitful. At times she became a distracting influence in class, but disciplining her through temporary exclusion proved entirely ineffective. She did not care if she was removed from the group. In addition, she had created a double-bind situation between herself and her peers. In an obvious effort to be accepted by them, she would tell extraordinary stories about things she had done. Her tales were so outlandish as to be obviously untrue, and her friends would accuse her of lying—which she would promptly deny, and then her friends would ignore her.

It was clear that the simple, natural, whole-bodily feeling of relational Happiness was missing in her life. She was unable to identify the feeling of Happiness and intimacy with others, and so excluding her from social contact was meaningless. In a conference with her parents, it became clear that the child was not feeling this nurturing Happiness with her parents. They provided their daughter with a disciplined routine but spent little intimate time with her.

The parents agreed to spend more time with her—real time, including outings and even a surprise stopover at Disneyland on a trip to southern California. Now the girl could take real pleasure in relating her true adventures to her friends. The change in the child was dramatic and immediate, and just as important, the parents were committed to persisting in the practice of intimacy with her over time.

On the basis of such consistent intimacy, temporary social exclusion of a child for negative or unrelational behavior can and does serve his or her social and spiritual adaptation.

Children should not be instructed about life and emotions primarily through language, or by being "talked at," nor should they be arbitrarily disciplined in the absence of prior intimacy. Rather, they should be instructed through intimacy, through the development of sensitivity to the primary emotion of love. Always enhance that sensitivity rather than deal problematically with secondary emotions. Children should be practicing the primary associative attitudes and experiences of serving, sharing, listening, touching, and so on.

What all this points to is that there are no "methods," no techniques for disciplining and raising children if you are not already loving. If you live this Way of life, the principles of creative human adaptation, including the discipline of children, will become obvious. In that case there will be no need for conventional techniques. The profound obligation to serve the highest adaptation of human growth will be your natural capability. Your service will be to God, not to fulfilling your own present and arbitrary requirements through loveless and willful demands. Your action, your body, and your speech will become ecstatic in your confession of the True Condition to your children. When you love there will be no failure to serve them in this Way of life.

Chapter 3

Surrender of the Body in God

a talk by Da Free John
August 11, 1980

M ASTER DA FREE JOHN: It is very easy to introduce a sex-negative, body-negative, and self-negative attitude in children through little punishment rituals, because we have all been indoctrinated in one way or another into a sex-negative, or at least an ambivalent, view of sexuality. On the one hand sex is affirmed, on the other hand it is denied. I can remember receiving basically sex-negative signals throughout my childhood. Sex was something you were not supposed to do unless you were married, but even then it was better if you didn't! (Laughter.) In the culture of my childhood, there was no systematic development of a positive body-sense relative to all one's functions. Therefore, in order to raise our children with a positive body-sense, everyone in our community must understand how he or she tends to reinforce a body-negative and sex-negative self-image, and then they must avoid dealing with children in those ways.

Children inevitably explore their bodies and feel them in various ways. To take the position that there is something wrong with all that is foolish. Nor do you have to make children explore and feel their bodies; they will do this naturally. When you find them doing it, what will be your response? You do not want to encourage habitual masturbating, but you also do not want to slap their hands and tell them that what they are doing is nasty or dirty. Rather, you must establish a more positive and ordinary education for children in which they become directly, feelingly, and sensually related to the world altogether. When they begin to notice things about their bodies, there should be no suppressive attack on them. That exploration is just a sign that they have reached a certain stage in self-observation, and you should help them. By the time they are capable of making such observations, they are usually old enough to engage in a discussion that will lead to an understanding of the body and its sensations.

As soon as children discover their bodies as terminals of sensation, they will tend to address them as instruments of sensation, and they will develop habits like masturbation and other kinds of private games, and in this way develop a dissociative character. The discovery of one's bodily and sexual sensations is obviously a positive aspect of children's development, and when children begin to make this discovery, we must lead them to an understanding that will make it unnecessary for them to choose to exploit the terminal of sensation in their own bodies. Instead, they should relate the body to the real world through sensual and perceptual awareness. By entering into that related connection to the world, the bodily energies attain a state of natural equanimity. However, as soon as individuals start stimulating the body for the sake of sensation, they develop a habitual mode of dissociation from others and from the world. They also get the idea that there is something wrong with bodily pleasure, that it is bad. So, their self-stimulation has to become secret. Generally, children who begin to exploit themselves sexually at an early age have sexual problems well into adulthood, until they are able to break out of the mode of privacy into sensual and sexual expression that is relational.

Therefore it is important that children in the first and second stages of life come to a positive understanding of their bodily discoveries. Instruction about sexuality and about the third or brahmacharya stage of life is useful. We should not cut children off, bodily, from life. Rather, we should lead them further into bodily forms of existence and perceptual association with the world. We should help them to develop an understanding of their sexual character and the sexual mechanism, and of how their early years are an initiation into the functions of the body in relationship to all kinds of potential experience. Sexuality has a great deal of learning associated with it. However, the fact that children are discovering sex as a possibility at an early age does not mean that they are ready for it.

Rather, at that point their cultural initiation must begin, and in this manner they will be prepared for the sexual yoga in their later married life.

It is helpful for children to be massaged throughout their years prior to marriage, and for them to massage others. This kind of bodily intimacy reinforces the positive sense of bodily existence. Thus, massaging, the development of unobstructed feeling, and positive bodily association with the world and with other people are all necessary aspects of character development.

A lot of what becomes the adolescent crisis is based on the discovery of one's own body as a terminal of experience, and that discovery occurs during childhood prior to the full development of relational life and relational experience. The usual adolescent, who is not drawn into the culture of such relational development and real learning, becomes reactive based on the principle of self-discovery. This is the root of the kind of obnoxious independence game that adolescents begin to exploit. This adolescent game of independence is based entirely on the discovery of the body as a principle of separative, egoic experience rather than a medium of association or relationship.

DEVOTEE: It seems that there would be different levels of instruction for children, based on the stages of life, which would specifically address the whole range of their life and functioning at different levels of maturity. And maybe there could also be a progressive teaching about how to relate to the Life-Force. For instance, children would learn about the awakening of the Life-Force in their own body, and then learn about it in relation to others, and, at a later stage, in regard to their marriage relationship.

MASTER DA FREE JOHN: Marriage is the ultimate fulfillment of one aspect of a process of learning that should have occurred all through life up to that point. In other words, the actual exercise of one's capacity for sexual experience comes only after a long period of learning and submission of the body into all relations, into the total field of experience in God. Children and teenagers who begin to exploit potentials for pleasure based on the self-principle, the body-principle independent of the development of a relational character, are people who have dissociative problems in later life.

You see, it is quite typical for teenagers and even younger children in the common world today to develop all kinds of ways of enjoying themselves through stimulation of the self-body. From early childhood and certainly from adolescence, they use intoxicants, drugs, alcohol, cigarettes, and forms of sexual exploitation. And when an individual has developed a culture of self-pleasure as profoundly as adolescents tend to develop it in our society, it becomes very difficult for them later on to live a harmonious life of relational culture, which is the obligation of mature humanity. For this reason, we must prevent the creation of a self-culture in childhood and adolescence. Until a person enters into the fourth stage of life, they should always be progressing in this general process of submitting the body to the field of relations in order to learn. Therefore, sexual activity should only begin after that preparation has taken place, and marriage is the ceremony of that initiation or ultimate development.

DEVOTEE: In the conventional society in which we grew up there was no sense of relationship at all. And so we turned to ourselves, our own bodies, to find pleasure. But in our spiritual culture, we live by a different principle.

MASTER DA FREE JOHN: Well, the self-body is the principle of conventional living because people are, in common society, basically dramatizing the level of development that is characteristic of the third stage of life, particularly the problematic development of that stage. Common society is basically an adolescent culture in which the self-body is the principle and everybody is, therefore, seeking some sort of self-enjoyment, self-fulfillment, and self-pleasure. The fullest dimension of their actual humanity does not have the opportunity to be expressed, because there is no culture or cultural demand for it. There is no demand for self-transcendence and submission of the body into the field of relations in God. That wisdom-culture is missing.

Thus, the self-body, rather than the surrender of the body in God and in all relationships, is the principle of conventional society. Therefore, conventional society is an adolescent, prehuman or subhuman culture. Human culture begins with the culture of the fourth stage of life. It is the culture that develops on the basis of the surrender of the whole body, or bodily surrender in God and in all relations. When the self-body itself becomes the principle of experience prior to the development of that elaborated relational culture, then the individual becomes fixed in the self mode, the Narcissistic culture of adolescence. And that is what typifies all of you! In fact, this description is characteristic of society in general. People are fixed in the principle of the self-body, and are therefore Narcissistic and dissociative and disturbed.

DEVOTEE: I think that is why it is difficult even to consider bringing this kind of premarital consideration to most teenagers. Because they have learned and adapted to so little wisdom in the earlier stages, talking about the "yoga of sexual communion" with them would be just like bringing them some kind of conventional sex instruction. If the whole emotional adaptation in relationship hasn't already occurred, they are not really prepared to enter into a mature consideration of human sexuality.

MASTER DA FREE JOHN: In our community, as children progress through the stages of growth, we must develop orderly forms of cultural experience that will make the period of life which becomes adolescence in the common world into a positive cultural epoch for each individual. This has traditionally been called the brahmacharya stage.

The third stage of life is not supposed to be adolescence! Adolescence is a crisis of reactive collapse upon the self-body and all of the problems, desires, and complications that accompany that collapse. The third stage of life, truly lived, is not expressed in the form of that adolescent crisis, but rather it is a life-positive, relation-positive period of learning and preparation for mature adult life and all of its conditions, including sexuality in marriage. But if specific and positive cultural circumstances are not provided for young people in that stage of life, they will tend to develop this adolescent crisis character, this Narcissistic orientation to the principle of the self-body.

Children are always tending to develop this Narcissistic character in one or another way throughout the first three stages of life.

Therefore, you must not make their discoveries of the self-body incidents for punishment and reinforcement of negative attitudes. Rather, consider them to be moments of learning, moments of increased awareness. Then, through that sense of awareness, lead the individual into the relational field of life—to greater sensitivity, energy, and attention for real growth rather than the exploitation of self. There is a natural and positive way to use all these incidents of self-discovery and the various events of developing childhood so that you do not suppress the personality of children and ultimately force them into an adolescent, self-involved crisis. Instead, you should enable them to become more life-positive, more sensitive, more expanded, more full of understanding and mature responsibility.

Chapter 4

Sila: The Discipline of Equanimity

a talk by Da Free John
April 1, 1983

MASTER DA FREE JOHN: Sila,[1] or equanimity, is a basic aspect of everyone's practice until the second stage of the Perfect Practice. Therefore, it is fundamental to the practice of children. The daily life of children should be altogether conducive to balance, ease, relaxation, and freedom from all the arbitrary, mechanical patterning that tends to develop when children are allowed to live sheerly on the basis of exploiting their vitality.

This exploitation of vitality is commonly called play or "playing around." You will notice that as soon as children play in this fashion they start getting a little wild. In fact, they get intoxicated with it. This is what outgoing exuberance is all about. It is a form of intoxication with desiring in the lower vehicle or lower coil[2] of life. This same intoxication occurs in the upper coil of life in the higher stages of practice, where people become fascinated with ascending energies. In either case, outgoing exuberance represents a form of enslavement to the outgoing movement of attention and energy.

Thus, sila, or equanimity, is fundamental. Even though there are many kinds of disciplines associated with the Way, there is one aspect that is of continuous significance throughout the course of spiritual

---

1. "Sila" is a Pali term meaning "habit, behavior, conduct." In the present context it denotes the restraint of outgoing energy and attention, the disposition of equanimity wherein energy and attention are free for the spiritual process.

2. The terms "lower coil" and "upper coil" have been explained on p. 41.

practice. That is this process of releasing energy and attention from the self-bond and of enjoying the state of equanimity, or natural control over the outgoing automaticities of energy and attention.

It is important, therefore, for adults to provide a way of life for children that is conducive to their development of this capacity. The community of practitioners has established a number of schools that are educating children in the first three stages of life, and my Teaching relative to education is a living consideration of how this should be done from the point of view of the Way of life in Truth. But because those who are educating these children were trained as educators in a worldly setting, and because the attitude of the adults in the community is still somewhat characteristic of middle-class, outgoing Americans, there is a tendency to undercut the spiritual principles in the education of our children.

Parents and teachers tend to think that they must constantly be stimulating young people, constantly providing ways to entertain them through field trips, sporting activities, and so on. They think that every day, for significant periods of time, they need somehow to interrupt the cycle of discipline, of peacefulness, ease, and naturalness, with stimulations that permit young people to indulge outgoing exuberance, the vital motive, or bondage to their conventional tendencies of attention.

This is a very worldly point of view. It has nothing to do with spiritual understanding. This form of indulgence will simply make children a duplicate of your own generation, which is not moved toward spiritual Realization. Even those of you who are now associated with a spiritual Way of life are having to go through a hard school of overcoming tendencies that you have been permitted to develop since your childhood. We should understand this and appreciate that an indulgent way of life is not fruitful. It does not produce a Happy human being capable of continued growth and spiritual Realization. It produces a retarded human being, an ego-based, worldly, troubled, and dependent personality who is always seeking Happiness in various conditions. Such a one is constantly aberrated, patterned into automaticities of energy and attention without control. We should understand and appreciate this completely and abandon that whole principle of indulgence. We must abandon it in our own case as practitioners, but we must also abandon it in the case of children and young people and create environments for their growth that will help them develop this capacity for equanimity.

It is not by constantly introducing children and youngsters to a circumstance of stimulated living that this capacity for equanimity is developed. In many ways, it is a matter of eliminating the interference represented by stimulation, fascination, "good times," and all the kinds of activity people in the world regard to be necessary for Happiness. Children should not be perpetually on retreat,[3] but their daily life should definitely prepare them for occasional retreats. Therefore, their daily life must be one that obliges them to exercise the capacity for equanimity, or control over outgoing exuberance.

Children must learn the discipline of sila, or responsibility for the movement of energy and attention, and be balanced and relaxed. This does not mean they can never have fun, but their basic mode of existence should be one that is balanced, relaxed, sympathetic to others and to the world, meditative, simple, and free. Therefore, whatever else adults do in educating children and young people, they should be constantly serving this disposition of equanimity. The discipline of sila would be served if schools were to offer a balanced, simple, orderly way of life, and not one in which every afternoon, or every weekend, there is some hyped up, stimulated event that the pupils look forward to. Their days should not consist of alternating periods of serious study and blowing it away out in the yard, you see. Nor should their life be the agitative life where children are constantly competing and quarrelling with one another. Rather, their life should be a much more simple, orderly, contained, balanced, sensitive, and truly Happy form of existence. That is what children must adapt to. That is the ideal that should be alive at The Garden of Lions and all other schools.

Once the culture of education has achieved that state, and once the children and youngsters in the schools have adapted to that disposition, then teachers can introduce useful or happy or amusing activities into their life circumstance wherever it is appropriate, without having to adopt the idea that in principle they are supposed to

---

3. The practice of retreat, engaged by children and adults alike, involves the setting aside of one's usual activities and relationships in a simplified environment for the sake of spiritual discipline.

be constantly stimulating them, "TV"-ing them, and all the rest of it. None of that stimulation is necessary. In fact, it is very destructive.

What will be the result, then, of individuals going through the three stages of education in this Way of life? Are they going to reach age eighteen or so and move out? Will they spend all the time they are a teenager just waiting for the day they can get out the gate, when they can come of age and go out and blow their minds? Will they want to do their thing in the world, simply because they have not realized the pleasure and the joy of the basic responsibility of equanimity and the spiritual disposition that grows only on that basis?

The discipline of equanimity should exist in a recognizable form in the school communities, and this form should also be evident in the households that are the children's environments after their day at school. Adult practitioners of this Way must begin to become sensitive to this obligation that is at the foundation of spiritual life. This Way of life is not a hyped, stimulated, worldly, middle-class way of living. Nor, however, do we starve ourselves to death. We are not ascetics who are obliged to be celibate and deprived.

This is a renunciate Way of life. It is a spiritual Way of life. It involves the free, intelligent discipline of functional existence, not its suppression. There can be occasional amusements—all the pleasures of existence are potential in such a disciplined Way of life. But its principle is spiritual in nature, and its practice is characterized by equanimity. In the midst of that Way of life and on the basis of that disposition, all of the varieties of human experience are possible and may be engaged truly and responsibly. The adult culture and the culture of children must take on the form that expresses this principle.

DEVOTEE: Master, having been on retreat with the children, I really appreciate what you say about our assumptions about what children are supposed to be doing. Living with them, observing and feeling them all the time, I know what they do that upsets their calm and balanced disposition. And the simplest way to keep them calm and balanced is, just as you said, to maintain a very structured form of life that is conducive to that disposition. I see how they can actually be quiet and alone for very long periods of time and by those means actually feel into Happiness, whereas when they are being vital, running around and playing, they do not have a clue to what Happiness is. Our assumption that as children they are supposed to play, run around, be noisy, and have a good time is our way of obstructing the spiritual process in them.

MASTER DA FREE JOHN: If your uninspected presumptions about what children should be allowed to do were indulged, the children would become duplicates of what you were before you became involved in this Way of life. Therefore, you must not indulge these uninspected presumptions. You must found yourself in the principles of this Way of life, understand it, and accept the discipline yourself. Then you must bring that same discipline, that same understanding, to the life of our children. They are our responsibility until they achieve a certain age, and thus we have the right and the obligation to create a circumstance of truly human and spiritual growth for them.

Chapter 5

The Culture of Expectation

based on a talk by Da Free John
June 20, 1981

Children must be "up against" themselves. They must be involved in self-transcendence. Unless parents begin to educate their children according to the principles of this Way in the early years of life, they will turn out to be the usual rebellious adolescents. Most of the time teachers and parents let the children "off the hook." Almost all children have a complete self-orientation, pursuing their own amusement, their own vitality, except when adults demand a little bit of them now and then. The discipline of self-transcendence must be obliged constantly! It is frequently being abandoned by children because parents and teachers abandon it themselves. Because the adults do not consistently bring the discipline to their own lives, they also do not bring it to the children. They tend to think that every child's life must be play, amusement, and pleasantries, but that is just the usual life of Narcissus.

The children's condition of existence must be one in which they are obliged to live with sensitivity. They must be obliged to be relaxed, they must be obliged to practice service in all relations, and they must be sensitive to and mindful of one another. They need to learn to serve others consistently as a real responsibility. Only occasionally should children be allowed play that engages their vitality vigorously. Of course, it is not that they should never have physical activities or play. But the kind of play in which they are allowed to be just little vital creatures should be available to them only like an occasional "dessert." As with adults, so with children. If adults do not enter seriously into the process of spiritual practice, then they will not oblige their children to do so either. Thus children tend to be happy little superficial egos who cannot be responsible when they are confronted with the real facts of existence. As soon as children begin to feel our demands or feel that life itself is a demand, then there is nothing but reactivity from them.

Children should express a feeling, quiet energy. Therefore, adults must introduce a "culture of expectation" for children and maintain it. And it <u>must</u> be maintained to be effective! They tend to think they are supposed to make life casually pleasant for children. This is not true. Every time a child dramatizes his or her particular strategy to gain the attention of others, he or she should be confronted with a definite expectation—an expectation that is not superficially enjoyable, so that the child will be made to see his or her own Narcissistic activity. Children must come to understand that they may be required to do things that they may not want to do. In other words, children must be given the structure in which to learn about both pleasure and pain. If children only lead a life of play, they will never be impressed by truly moral circumstances, nor will they be impressed with the total world of the Divine Reality. They will not see significant things about themselves—except their vital game—and this does not serve them. The being grows through confrontation, difficulty, and demand. Children are very repetitive. They repeat the same vital games day after day. Where are the new signs of their adaptation, where is their higher growth?

We must be consistent in our service to children all day long. There must be this true or moral demand. Never step aside from it. If we consistently change our expectations of children, they will not change! Introduce requirements and discipline children if they do not meet them. Do this in the midst of a life of loving intimacy, for intimacy is the healing principle. Children must learn to be calm all day long, whatever they are doing. Adults make them stressful by allowing or encouraging them to lead a self-oriented vital life, and in this sense their play is disturbed. Calmness is pleasant; whole-body feeling is pleasurable. Children's wild, vital play is actually disturbing them, and they become dependent on feeling disturbed. They feel it is necessary for happiness, whereas it is a calm, balanced, feeling life that is truly pleasurable. We must help children become sensitive to other people and teach them how to cooperate and serve in all their relations. Also, children should learn to bring feeling and sensitivity to the meditative exercise, as given in *What to Remember to Be Happy*, and to other devotional practices appropriate to their stage of life. These activities serve the process of the child's relationship to the Mystery of existence.

One child recently boasted, "I am supposed to remember the names of the characters in the Disney book *One Hundred and One Dalmatians*." Children should not be given such trivial education. An assignment such as this is the equivalent of junk food in the diet. Thus far, their diet is actually better than their moral training. This random moral instruction of them is the equivalent of junk food, whereas they should be talking about spiritual life, about the Mystery. They should be talking and learning about spiritual Teachers, and studying moral, religious, and spiritual stories. Children should be introduced, constantly and all day long, to a non-ordinary way of life. Find a way to make their lessons be aligned to the Teaching of Truth and with this spiritual Way of life. Their lessons should have moral and spiritual significance, and children should not be instructed in a way that merely impresses them, but that truly awakens their understanding.

Another common misunderstanding relative to children is that parents and teachers often think children are supposed to feel that they are the center of everyone's life, almost to the point where they begin to think they are the center of the universe. There is no reason why anybody should have that tendency reinforced. Even at a very young age there is no cause for children to think they are the center of everyone's world. They must be brought into relational force with others. They must be served to move out of their independent self-involvement into the condition of relationship.

My Teaching as it applies to education has been available for many years, but it has not been used. The situation of children in the community is the same as that of the adult practitioners. The instructions are very clear, but nothing changes. Parents and teachers will sit down with their children and talk to them every now and then, and have occasional serious considerations with them, but they never communicate to them a consistent cultural expectation. Thus, their moral teaching is only "dessert" to the children and is not really taken into account. It is only a momentary diversion from the child's life of vitalizing.

In the usual life of children everything is play, and they are very lazy when it comes to service. There is an inconsistent demand placed on them without proper consequences for their actions. They are constantly involved with their superficial egoic dramas, instead of being calm, considerate individuals. In a traditional setting children would attend a brahmacharya school and live a completely regimented life under very severe discipline, with play as an occasional diversion. In modern American society, play is a way of life. The ultimate ideal is to be totally self-involved and even make your living out of being self-involved.

In traditional spiritual societies, however, play was considered a "dessert." Teachers and parents fail to understand this. They constantly return to the "life-as-play" idea. Because their demands are not consistent, the children escape the edge of discipline necessary for true human growth. Children should not be permitted to casually leap around and vitalize. That kind of play should be a "dessert." The basic life of a child should be quiet and sensitive. It should be a learning process, an intuitive life of positive feeling and free energy and attention. If children's intuitive capacity is developed at an early age, they will not suffer from, and have to deal with, the usual self-centered orientation in their later lives.

There should not be a lot of wild, vital play. Children do not know anything about true play! We have to consciously introduce them to play. We have to teach them in a way that is a balanced expression of whole-body equanimity. Otherwise children use play as a form of self-possession.

Unfortunately, parents and teachers bring this kind of discipline to children only occasionally, whereas it must be maintained constantly. It must be obliged all day long. A child's life should not be anything that adults are committed to in their own childish and adolescent strategies. Adults as well as children are committed to vital stimulation, amusement, and distraction; this is the way most people are driven to live. It is already a big deal for people to put aside an hour for meditation. Therefore, meditation cannot serve any useful purpose, because as soon as the hour is over they either return to their stressful life of "getting things done" or to their self-indulgence of random vitalizing. Thus, no real energy is brought to the practice of spiritual life or to the creation of true community.

If adults fail to bring this discipline to their own lives and to their children, then they give their children no gift. If there is no discipline of expectation for children, then adults are performing a total disservice to them. In the life of every child there must be calmness, sensitivity, and behavioral appropriateness. And the key to the fulfillment of this expectation is to vigorously maintain it all day long, every day, throughout the childhood years. Only then is the child's energy and attention free to feel and participate in the Mystery of existence.

There is a basic principle that should be the underlying structure in the life of every child: Strict cultural discipline, maintained consistently for a very long time. During childhood that is basically how children should be served. Their casual play and vitalizing should be restricted in a disciplined culture of expectation, while they learn to fully adapt to the responsibilities of the second and third stage and the laws of mature human life. People have to make a turnabout relative to the way they serve their children and what they expect their lives to be. If you were to maintain this discipline over many years, you would see a profound change in the children—but it has to be maintained. If people would seriously approach this Teaching and use the wisdom that is given, then a very different level of maturity can emerge in the lives of their children.

Unfortunately, people do not want to deal rigorously with themselves. They want life to be a constant diversion, not a discipline. And when they choose a life of discipline, they tend to spend most of their time with their reactions. People have to learn how to generate discipline from their own Place. Instead of being hyperactive and exploiting life, they have to become sensitive, calm, and observant. This is the best way for an adult to live, and likewise it is the best way to raise and educate children. Establish a disciplined spiritual culture of expectation, and oblige children to its demands and responsibilities. Otherwise, by the time they are twenty, they will only be self-involved chippies and punks, like every other self-centered adolescent, suffering and screaming their brains loose. Why bring them up for that?

Chapter 6

Spiritual Life Is the
Real Principle of Order

a talk by Da Free John
February 25, 1983

MASTER DA FREE JOHN: I want you to understand the real principles involved in this matter of community. Basically they are extensions of the same principles on which to base individual practice. Individual practice is a matter of hearing, seeing, and practicing.[1] Traditionally, this process is conceived as consisting of four steps, the fourth being Realization. But in this Way of life, the spiritual process is not based on a problem-conception, on a presumed disease, and therefore the Realization of Truth is not the goal or the end phenomenon of our spiritual exercise, but rather its foundation from the very beginning.

I interpret hearing and seeing and therefore practicing in a different light from the one that is common to the traditions. Hearing, seeing, and practicing are themselves all about Realizing. Realizing does not merely occur at the end of a long period of practice, but is consistent with every aspect of the Way, coincident with every

---

1. "Hearing" and "seeing" are technical terms used by Master Da Free John to describe the conscious and spiritual Awakenings that are the necessary foundation of the Way that he Teaches. "Hearing" is the intuitive understanding of the self-contraction and simultaneous intuitive awakening to Divine Consciousness that arise on the basis of disciplined study of the Argument of the Adept. Hearing leads naturally to "seeing," which is emotional and total bodily awakening into faith, or direct feeling-intuition of the Divine Reality under all circumstances. Master Da has also described seeing as conversion from self-possession to God-Communion in, as, and through all relations and all phenomenal experience. Only on the basis of continual hearing and seeing can the practice of true spiritual life begin. Such practice is generated not as a means to Truth but on the basis of prior understanding.

moment of the Way. Thus, I conceive practice in terms of three stages: hearing, seeing, and practicing, or in other words, understanding, reception of the Spirit-Blessing, and the life expression founded on prior self-understanding and meditation. Just as individual practice develops in this way, so also the collective or cultural practice develops in those three stages.

The creation of a brahmacharya school or an ashram for young people is really just a special version of the creation of community or of a household. It is a special version of the process of creating a Sanctuary, a Hermitage, or a public Center.[2] In other words, a brahmacharya school is not just a place where adults superimpose an ideal of some sort on a bunch of young people in order to control their behavior. The point is not merely to try to generate superficial, worldly religiosity in children, nor is it merely to make them socially functional beings. The principle that is fundamental to an ashram or a spiritual community is not the form or the control of behavior itself.

One of the basic problems in the community schools at the present time is that the fundamental principles of this Way of life and of any genuine spiritual community are not yet real enough in the daily life and practice. Instead, what is happening in those schools is basically a struggle on the part of adults to somehow create order and discipline, and they are encountering problems in trying to do this. The young people in the ashram schools do not have the resources in themselves to simply live an orderly way of life. They have all kinds of aberrated tendencies and interests. Their outgoing exuberance, their vitality just wants to wing it, have fun, and be free of controls. Thus, the adults who run these schools are stuck with two options. They can try to control behavior and to systematize life and so forth, but they will discover that this fails to one or another degree. The young people are not comfortable with it; they backslide, or even find this to be an

---

2. The term "Sanctuaries" here refers to sites maintained by The Free Daist Communion for use by practitioners as places of retreat. Sanctuaries also house empowered temple sites accessible according to maturity in practice. The Hermitage is a renunciate Sanctuary provided for use by Heart-Master Da and for those who serve his intimate circumstance. Centers are the central places for educational and spiritual gatherings in each region of the United States and elsewhere where his devotees congregate, practice in community, and make the Teaching of the Way of Radical Understanding available to all others.

artificial limit on their behavior and therefore would have a legitimate complaint about it. Then the adults can play the other option and try to appear less like parental authorities. They may grant the young people more freedom and presumed responsibility. But they tend to become soft and permissive, and end up allowing the children to do whatever they want. The game then goes back and forth between these two extremes. On the one hand, a system of control or order is created resembling a strict Catholic boarding school, and on the other hand more liberality and freedom is granted, as at Summerhill or a Montessori school.

The adults are playing on the problem of behavior and order. This is like introducing the principle of practice before you have introduced the principles of hearing and seeing. In other words, teachers will never be able to create a true cultural order, one that is creatively alive and really useful to young people, until they begin to found their daily life and their lives altogether in the real practice of the foundation principles of this Teaching. Everyone in an ashram school should base his or her life on self-understanding and meditation, and then, on the basis of the free disposition, or the equanimity of self-understanding and meditation, move into the form or predictable order of ashram life.

Summerhill, you see, was not a spiritual community. The Montessori approach to education is not based on a spiritual way of life either. These approaches to education and many other so-called modern liberal approaches are not rooted in a spiritual point of view. They are based on a reaction to the traditional approach to education, on the observation that that approach was founded, as secular education generally is, on behavioral training (or so-called moral and social training) and technical learning (which is just a matter of doing schoolwork and absorbing information).

The modern approaches conceive of the traditional orientation as simply a way of controlling, robotizing, and armoring people. Montessori, for instance, was very sensitive to what happened to the general populace during Hitler's reign in Germany and wanted to find out why people were prone to such blindly obedient behavior. She found fault with the education system that simply controlled people and made them passive. Thus, her own more liberal approach was meant to correct this shortcoming. Although there is undoubted virtue in the modern liberal approaches to education, they often represent merely the opposite extreme of the views criticized by them. In this respect, they are just the other side of the coin.

There are some virtues in a rather strict approach to education, as embodied in the Catholic system, the old school system, and so forth. There are some virtues in the approach of Neill at Summerhill, of Montessori, Steiner, Dewey, and others. In other words, there are some virtues in both the liberal and conservative approaches to education, but none of these approaches is sufficient in itself and none of them is founded on the spiritual principle.

If the spiritual principle is consistently applied, then you will naturally discover how to live together. But you will not solve the problem of creating a rational way of life with other people until you have dealt with the Truth. This matter of the Truth or a spiritual Way of life cannot merely be some ideal that you kick around in conversation, or try to superimpose on yourself and others. The Truth must be made the very principle of your life.

The Truth does not imply either a liberal or a conservative approach to existence. Rather, the Truth should be the basis of our approach to existence. And I am not talking about Truth in the abstract, as an ideal or a conception in which we simply believe. I am talking about the Truth in practice, the matter of self-understanding and meditation, lived as the basic ground of your existence. If you cannot hear (or understand yourself), if you cannot see (or receive the Spirit-Blessing and begin to meditate and to enter into Divine Communion), then you cannot be expected to practice either. And if you cannot practice, you cannot create a community, an ashram, or a school. In summary then, the principle of Truth as self-understanding and meditation must be fundamental to the daily life of every student and teacher—from the time they get up in the morning until they go to sleep. Instead, they wake up as egos and then have the obligation to live together and create some sort of order that corresponds to or looks like a spiritual way of life.

To enter into community, to enter into the practice of the disciplines of spiritual life, you must first hear and see. You must first understand yourself, meditate, and enter into Divine Communion, and allow that to transform your existence by establishing equanimity, opening the mind, releasing the free energy of the Divine Being, enlarging or transfiguring you in some real sense—emotionally, mentally, and physically. On that basis you can then observe the disciplines, live a life of service, and engage in community life. Then, only after the principles of hearing and seeing are established, can you truly adapt to spiritual practice altogether, which includes the various disciplines as well as life in community.

Before a brahmacharya school, an ashram, a community household, a Sanctuary, or a Center can be created, you must first fulfill the same obligations that you must also meet in your practice in general. You cannot create these social structures unless you are established in the principles of hearing and seeing, understanding and meditation. Once you are established in these principles, then you will intuitively know what kind of culture of daily life should be created.

It is rather simple to understand the Teaching in principle, just as it is simple to understand in principle what the practice should be altogether. You know what the practices are in personal terms. They are straightforward practices of diet, exercise, health, sexuality, and the relational life of service and cooperation. In other words, the disposition founded on hearing and seeing tends to express itself through all the forms of equanimity, and would therefore tend to express itself also in the form of order. Thus, a spiritual community or an ashram is naturally characterized by order and formality, but order and formality are not themselves the principle. Where the real principles are established, where hearing and seeing, or self-understanding and meditation, are the basis of daily life, then one can expect that practitioners will express or magnify that hearing and seeing through the form of order, and that order becomes community, ashram, household life, and so on.

Where these real principles are not established, order is almost impossible to create except through the use of power or outside influence. Then, if a person conforms or obeys, he is rewarded; if he does not, he is punished. That is how it works in the world in general. That is politics. When people are not established in the Truth, the only way to establish order is through power, and if power is not used, then people tend to act rather chaotically.

And so it is in an ashram or a spiritual community. If individuals are not established in the Way itself in their moment to moment existence, then the natural order that should be present in a spiritual community is always in doubt. It is something you are always struggling to create by trial and error.

You will tend to create very strict programs, but the people involved are not free in themselves: They are ego-based and have a lot of excess vitality and outgoing exuberance which are not really controllable by any regime of outer demands. Such a regime only suppresses and rigidifies people. In other words, after a while you recognize that creating order by laying down the law does not work. Then you try it the other way. You give people more freedom or responsibility, but responsibility is not something that can merely be assigned. A person must have the capacity for responsibility. Sooner or later you find that this alternative does not work either. When people are given freedom without having the capacity for responsibility, they tend to indulge in their aberrations.

Whether you tighten up or loosen your control, impediments will always occur, because the ego is the basis of life for all those involved. You are then dealing with people who are not established in the Truth, that is to say, who are not established in the fundamental principles of the Way, which would express themselves as order if they were truly lived.

In the setting of a brahmacharya school, which is an Ashram for young people in the third stage of life, there ideally would be a predictable scheme of what you do from the time you get up until the time you go to bed—every day of the year. Within that basic scheme there would, of course, be certain days and certain occasions that are somewhat different. Some days there would not be schooling, some days there would be celebrations, and some days there would be one or another form of entertainment. But, as a rule, the basic order would be maintained. Since this depends on cooperative behavior, true fulfillment of life within the context of this order would be positively reinforced. This reinforcement would not take the form of "receiving a piece of candy for doing the dishes." Rather, it would take the form of positive feelings from others, of the general enjoyment of life, and the sharing of energies which occurs when you live within the agreed framework.

In a brahmacharya school, as at any ashram or Center, there would need to be at least a few practitioners who are highly skilled in serving people in spiritual terms and who can maintain this cultural order. This order would be the expected way of life in an ashram. The way of life would include: arising early in the morning, sitting in meditation for a time, perhaps participating in various sacred activities—sacramental services, recitations, and so on—exercise, meals, various kinds of service time, schooling time, meditation again later in the day, certain kinds of evening gatherings, and retirement by a certain time. That is what it would be throughout the year, and without a three-month summer vacation. Three months' vacation every summer is a negative factor in people's education. It cuts the thread, you see. It interrupts the whole course of study, and there is no need for it at all. Schooling would be a three-hundred-and-sixty-five-day-a-year process, and it would begin before kindergarten.

There would be some days every week or every month when students do not study, but these would not be times of license or separation from the cultural environment. They would simply be times in which the routine is not associated with schoolwork. There could also be longer breaks, perhaps extending over a week or more, but these too would not involve separation from the culture of daily life. They would merely be a break from regular study. One appropriate time for the longer breaks to occur would be during celebration times that take place every two months.[3] This would permit the young people to participate in these larger cultural events. But there would be a regular orderly life in a brahmacharya school and all other schools, and there would also be right positive reinforcement for living those conditions. It should not be anything like reinforcing rats who are trying to learn a maze. Rather, what I am saying to you is that this kind of life is impossible, unenjoyable, and unendurable by people who are not spiritual practitioners and who do not enjoy a spiritual Way of life.

There is no question that order should exist. In that sense, a rather conservative approach to spiritual culture is appropriate,

---

3. The Johannine Daist Communion annually enjoys six major Celebrations. Three of these commemorate historic events in the life and Teaching Work of Master Da Free John, and the remaining three acknowledge his Presence, Teaching, and Way during times of traditional spiritual celebration.

although there should be a lot of leeway and creative potential in it. It should not have the qualities of a strict Catholic school education with all the punishment games, physical abuses, and mere indoctrination of resistive children who are not given the wisdom to understand themselves and to really practice. It is not about making people merely passive and submissive and hammering their energies down. But it is not like the liberal approach either, in which children are considered to be something like shorter adults who just follow their own inner movement and do basically what they like with very little outer control or limit on their actions.

What makes this relatively conservative approach to cultural life work? The answer is spiritual practice—hearing and seeing, or self-understanding and meditation engaged as the most fundamental aspect of daily life. Every day should begin with spiritual practices, some done in private, others engaged collectively.

The third stage of life is not merely the last few years of childhood, after which you go out and confuse yourself in the usual adult fashion and then decide whether or not you want to live a spiritual life. Children, especially third stagers, are quite capable of choosing a spiritual life. We are not merely superimposing some sort of arbitrary culture on children. We are making it possible for them to participate in the living Truth and to consider spiritual wisdom in their own terms at each stage of life. It is not merely that they are naive and we can indoctrinate them and then keep them in our community all their lives, or have them come to a point of legal freedom so they can abandon it. Spiritual life is as choosable in childhood as it is at any other stage of life. And what adults should be doing is making it possible for their children to have access to real spiritual life so that they can in fact choose it. Then their choice and their practice will permit them to be involved in a spiritual Way of life all their lives.

The adult practitioners of this Way of life are not suffering from the absence of a Teaching or a Teacher. They are suffering all the evidence of egoity, of the non-use of the Teaching and the Teacher. You are not merely supposed to worship the Teaching and the Teacher in cultic terms. You are not supposed to be egos who say,

"Oh, what a great man!" and "Oh, what a great Teaching!"

You abstract me, objectify me, make me into a kind of ideal figure, to be used as an instrument of your imagination when you are looking for consolation. Instead of really using me, entering into Communion with me, with the Divine in my Company, you make me into this abstracted other who is the subject of praise, but just as often the subject of abuse.

I see this sort of "Do it for the Gipper, do it for the Spiritual Teacher" approach. This is a wrong kind of attachment. It is cultic. It is not the right, formal, and truly devotional association with me that is expressed by people who are practicing. It is the expression of people who are, instead, trying to get themselves interested in practicing by holding up this image. It is a little bit like the pictures we had of Jesus when I was a child in Sunday School—with the robe, the long hair, a sheep under one arm, and patting a child on the head. To encourage children to turn to me in this sense would certainly not be the right approach. They should be practicing spiritual life. They have direct access in their own Place to That which I Am, That which I Give to them, and That which I have made accessible to them. It is on the basis of their Communion with That that they should develop an involvement with me, a response to me. The only true response is the one that comes out of real practice.

When people do not practice, do not understand themselves, do not meditate, and do not have direct access to the Spiritual Reality, they develop a false and cultic relationship to the Teacher which tends to be full of false, gleeful praise and therefore abuse. I begin to be treated like a parent, and people become involved in transference games, just as they do with their psychiatrists. They transfer the image of a parent or super-other to the psychiatrist, together with all the emotions associated with that image. Thus, they play out romances with the psychiatrist, dependence and independence games. They love the psychiatrist, they hate the psychiatrist. And for what is the psychiatrist supposed to be there? He is supposed to help you understand yourself and transcend your limitations. And that is what I am supposed to be here for, not to be party to your cultism or your transference games. I am not here to be a psychiatrist, either. I am here to be an Agent of Spiritual Transmission. But I can be such an Agent only for those who practice, who understand themselves, and who have access in their own Place to the Spiritual Reality that I awaken in them and make accessible to them.

Table 1

Conscious Discipline in the First Three Stages of Life

FIRST STAGE (Birth to 7) Vital-Physical Adaptation	SECOND STAGE (Years 7-14) Emotional-Sexual Adaptation	THIRD STAGE (Years 14-21) Mental-Intentional Adaptation
Discipline is *physically* based.	Discipline is *emotionally* based.	Discipline is based on *understanding, discrimination,* and *will.*
1. Create the child's incident from moment to moment.	1. Encourage self-generated responsibility through clear guidelines and positive reinforcement.	1. Help the teenager to become fully responsible for the functions of the body-mind.
2. Cultivate bodily intimacy.	2. Encourage the child to move into self-transcending service.	2. Help to awaken in the young person an understanding of the principles of human existence and spiritual life.
3. Do not talk and moralize—act!	3. Enter into agreements and grant rights and privileges based on the child's maturing responsibility.	3. Allow the teenager to learn from the natural consequences of his or her actions, and grant access to greater cultural freedom on the basis of the young person's demonstrated responsibility for the functions of human life.
4. Use loving force to move the child bodily into a different disposition. Clearly define limits.	4. Encourage the positive expression of emotion as love, and attract the child to right action rather than focus on his or her "problem."	4. Encourage the young person to expand his or her intimacy to the whole community, and assume a relationship of compassionate friendship rather than continuing to play parent-child roles.
5. Teach the child to release negativity through the breath cycle—"breathe in the good stuff, breathe out the bad stuff"—and remind the child that he or she can be Happy in any given moment on the basis of this simple breathing.	5. Awaken the child to the disposition of blessing others through positive speech, thought, and action, and help the child to experience the breath process, his or her emotional life, and the entire realm of Nature *as* energy.	5. Assist the teenager to develop the earlier exercises of breathing and feeling as energy into the formal practice of conductivity, and encourage him or her to learn to transcend emotional reactivity and negativity through the practice of the conscious process and conductivity.

Table 2

The Three Forms of Intimacy in Childhood

A child is helped to pass through the crises of growth and new adaptation at every stage through three functional forms of development, which are forms of intimacy:

1. Bodily Intimacy with Human Relations
Expressed via service: The giving of energy and attention in all relationships.

2. Bodily Intimacy with the World of Nature
Expressed via freedom of movement and association with the elemental world.

3. Bodily Intimacy with God (The Mystery, or Divine Reality)
Expressed via meditation and the reception-release cycle of the feeling breath.

These three forms of intimacy are not hierarchical. In other words, a child should *not* first relate only to the matrix of human relations (particularly the mother), then begin to associate with the matrix of the world of Nature, and then finally, on that basis, begin to associate with the Divine Reality or Mystery of existence. From infancy a child should be brought into forms of bodily intimacy with *all three* aspects of existence. The third aspect—the Divine Reality or Mystery—is the senior principle, and pervades and influences the domains of human and natural relations. *The Divine Reality or Mystery is the primary matrix of association in which every child should learn the art of bodily intimacy.*

Thus, the key to raising a child according to the highest wisdom is to establish the process of bodily Happiness in the child's life. Teach the child how to keep energy and attention in Happiness, or the "feeling of the Mystery," at all times.

Table 3

The True Principles of Children's Discipline

Conventional Punishment vs. Conscious Discipline

Conventional Punishment	Conscious Discipline
1. Is an expression of annoyance, frustration, and anger.	1. Is an expression of blessing and bodily Happiness.
2. Generates animosity and rebellion.	2. Generates self-discipline and personal responsibility.
3. Is founded on reactivity and the sense of the child as inferior.	3. Is based on agreements and mutual commitments.
4. Binds energy and attention through problems and dilemmas.	4. Frees up available energy and attention for growth.
5. Is self-referring.	5. Is self-transcending.
6. Is inflexible and tends to remain the same.	6. Takes new forms as the child matures.
7. Is oriented to a problem-solution dilemma based on the history of the child's past action.	7. Is oriented to the child's right action in the present.
8. Adapts the child to the "life-as-threat" idea.	8. Adapts the child to lawful conditions of life.
9. Is a bodily demonstration of forceful un-love.	9. Is a bodily demonstration of forceful love.
10. Is a form of *verbal* attack, employing both moralizing and lecturing.	10. Is a form of *positive action*.
11. Imposes arbitrary demands unrelated to the incident as consequences for inappropriate behavior.	11. Relates consequences for inappropriate behavior to the actual incident.
12. Expresses the demand of adult authority and personal power of parent and teacher.	12. Expresses the demand of the wisdom culture of higher human maturity.
13. Confuses the child and teaches him opposing values.	13. Establishes the child in a condition of equanimity and understanding.
14. Is used as a method to be applied only when the child misbehaves.	14. Is realized as a life-positive disposition, or whole Way of life.
15. Is to make sure the child understands how "bad" he is.	15. Is to "look and feel and be and act completely Happy."
16. Orients the child to self and subjectivity.	16. Orients the child to the Mystery, or Divine Reality.
17. Promotes the attitude of separation.	17. Expresses the commitment to relationship.

Table 4

Practical Guidelines—At a Glance

True discipline awakens the child to the feeling dimension of his or her being, and this allows the child to become aware of the Mystery of existence in terms of a whole-bodily feeling. Whenever a child in the first two stages of life (up to approximately age fourteen) has an unhappy episode or is dramatizing reactive emotions, the following simple steps can serve as guidelines for bringing him or her back into relationship and feeling-awareness of the Mystery of life. However, these instructions should *not* be followed mechanically. Rather, they must be applied in the context of intimacy: The adult must be in wholehearted relationship to the child when applying discipline.

1. Bring the child into intimate bodily relationship (though not necessarily bodily contact).

2. Ask, "What are you feeling?" and allow the child to express his or her feelings simply, without making any comments or judgments yourself.

3. Ask, "Is that feeling Happiness?" and wait for a response.

4. Ask the child to do the Feeling-Breathing Technique: (a) "Breathe up from the bottoms of your feet to the top of your head"; (b) "Feel that *you* can relax"; (c) "Smile from the inside or from your heart."—Do this with the child until equanimity is reestablished.

5. Ask, "Now that you feel Happy in the Mystery, what are you going to do?" and let the child determine the appropriate action of coming back into relationship in the situation.

Never do any of the following:

1. Make degrading comments ("I can't believe you are doing this again").

2. Make righteous demands ("Why don't you stop being so silly and just be happy!").

3. Enter into a complicated abstract consideration of the practice.

4. Make judgments about what the child is doing ("This is completely inappropriate!").

5. Threaten the child ("If you don't do what I tell you, I am going to punish you").

6. Preach and moralize ("This isn't the way to live. You should not do this, you should do that, etc., etc.).

Always observe any feelings on your part of superiority, reactivity, or needing to *control* children's behavior.

"Do not make children pay the price of a wounded psyche."
                                        Master Da Free John

PART III

LOVE
IS THE
GREAT
MYSTERY

INTRODUCTION TO PART III

In his widely read book *Understanding Media*,[1] Marshall McLuhan made the astute observation that most people suffer from the "rearview mirror" syndrome: Their glance is fixed on the past, and therefore they do not see where they are going. McLuhan applied this metaphor specifically to the failure to understand the significance of the media, but it can just as usefully be applied to people's attitude toward life in general. They have very little self-understanding and hence rather blindly live out their short span on earth. They do not recognize the full, awesome, and magnificent potential of the human being and so tend to fritter away their lives with frivolous diversions and consoling occupations. And because they see nothing wrong with their diminished way of life, they bring up their children in the same fashion—thus replicating a pattern of existence which is euphemistically called "civilization" but which has moved mankind to the brink of subhumanness and extinction.

Master Da Free John speaks of the "spell of childish and subhuman persuasions"[2] which must be broken if there is to be a future for humanity. He goes on to show how this can be done:

> *Individuals must be instructed, initiated, and obliged to adapt to the higher human wisdom and its ways. They must be awakened from the childhood visions of fearful dependency, and the adolescent ways of egocentric exploitation of independent and private experience. My Work in the world is, at base, an initiatory influence of this kind.*
>
> *The superior or mature human being must become the goal of our adaptation and, thus, of all the educational influences we promote.[3]*

1. M. McLuhan, *Understanding Media: The Extensions of Man* (New York: Signet Books, 1964).
2. Da Free John, *Love of the Two-Armed Form*, p. 26.
3. Ibid, pp. 26–27.

Compared to this great, inspiring vision, conventional education—even of the avant-garde type—represents no more than a timid compromise with our secularized society, which equates Enlightenment with left-brained knowledge. Conventional education, at its very best, addresses three areas of functional adaptation to life—thinking (cognitive education), feeling (affective education), and living in community (social education). For the most part, however, contemporary education is designed to turn out left-brained "knowers" who have imbibed the (largely useless) knowledge prescribed by the school or university curriculum. Ideally, they are good problem-solvers, but in reality, they tend to be pitifully inadequate in simple human terms.

Even so-called religious education barely improves on this situation. In fact, it can be said to aggravate it by superimposing on all this learning an archaic belief in a Parental Deity who sits (uneasily) in the gaps of human knowledge. This belief, or God-idea, merely caters to the neurotic trait of childish dependency, which belongs to the personality make-up of many, if not most, people. And the rebelliously independent types—representing another form of neurosis (or self-possession)—are likely to discard this naive theology together with the moral teaching that religions have to offer.

Meantime, progressive educators are searching for viable alternatives that will free mankind from the shackles of dogmatism and authoritarianism. However, their concept of freedom suffers the same shortcomings as their notion of potential human growth: They appear to be oblivious to the possibility of *perfect* self-transcendence in the form of God-Realization. Talk about human freedom only makes sense in the context of Man's higher evolutionary destiny. Outside an authentic culture of spiritual realization, freedom is only an illusion. Criticizing the popular understanding of the democratic ideal, Master Da Free John remarks:

Human freedom is not in principle about the ability to randomly fulfill random desires. The true principle of human freedom is a higher cultural concept of the status of superior human individuals, not childish masses of vulgar subhumanity. Human freedom is a mature realization of the status of individual existence in relationship with all other human beings and all aspects of the shared world. Human freedom is a political or relational estate, rather than a separately personal one. It is the disposition in which the higher or evolutionary conditions of one's superior adaptation are chosen, and in which full moral responsibility is accepted for one's social and intimate relationships.[4]

Ultimately, human freedom is the Freedom of Spontaneous Existence as a fully human being. "Man," states Master Da Free John, "is subhuman until he Awakens from mere desire, or self-indulgence, to Love, or self-transcendence, in constant Communion with the Living God and in Lawful or responsible management of all functional and relational conditions of experience."[5] The Awakened being, the God-Realizer, Realizes that he is, and always has been, inherently Free. "We cannot cease to be Free,"[6] says Master Da Free John. But this insight must become one's literal Truth.

Spiritual practice is a sustained effort to Realize this prior Freedom, which is perfect Spontaneity, perfect Happiness. It is a process by which that insight, or intuitive premise, is Magnified until it breaks through as a literal Realization. This requires that one live from the viewpoint of one's prior Freedom and Happiness. This is possible only when one liberates energy and attention from their usual fixations, through a disciplined (not repressive) Way of life. Then, in moments of free energy and attention, or real self-transcendence, that Freedom or Happiness is immediately obvious.

Over time, the body-mind will become readapted until, at the unsurpassable culmination of the educational process, the practitioner is overtaken by the ultimate event of Enlightenment, or perpetual Ecstatic Self-Abiding in Happiness and Freedom. At that point a new, Spontaneous form of education begins in which the Enlightened being gradually Transforms his bodily and relational existence by Incarnating the undiminishable Love-Bliss that is his Identity. This is not an experience or a form of knowledge. It is a permanent condition, *the* Condition of all the busy processes of life. It is an unresolvable Paradox, a great Mystery.

4. Da Free John, *Scientific Proof of the Existence of God Will Soon Be Announced by the White House!* p. 68.

5. Ibid., p. 88.

6. Ibid., p. 398.

Chapter 7

The Practice of Ecstasy
with Children

based on a talk by Da Free John
March 29, 1979

I n our society, children are not generally taught to live with God. What are they taught, then? What are they given? They are given the whole world of TV and all of the popular storybooks. They are obsessively involved with storybook characters and images that are not in any way created from the point of view of Enlightenment. Rather, these characters are duplicates of the problematic state of human beings in their unillumined condition. Our children are thus randomly associated with the imagery of a worldly consciousness.

We do not even presume it appropriate to pass on to them as archetypes of a real and Godly life the mythologies of Divine association from the traditions of religion and spirituality. Generally, we indoctrinate our children with a fake mythology of unreal characters like Santa Claus and "the Hulk." Clearly, such unreal characters must not be the archetypes by which our children are inspired. We must teach them about association with the Divine. Thus, we may read them stories, but these should be interpreted from the disposition of association with God. Give them the opportunity to live with a mythology based on Reality, on real people, spiritual figures and devotees, incarnations of God.

Children should not hear or read stories simply to be entertained by them, but to be obliged to a moral understanding. Therefore, when you tell children a story, you must require them to make a response.

Stories for children should be associated with moral and spiritual learning. Children must learn what a spiritual relationship is. They must recognize the Spirit-Power that literally is contacted through feeling and breathing. They must learn that that Power is the Divine. Therefore, instead of playfully allowing them to become motivated to play out the games of threat and fear that they encounter in conventional stories, orient them to a Life-positive understanding and practice. We must try to teach children to live a happy and positive way of life through all of their functions.

Children generally communicate and dramatize that they feel threatened. They typically rehearse their future adult consciousness by identifying with threatened personalities. We must teach them to dramatize an unthreatened consciousness instead. Only from the unthreatened point of view can they overcome the difficult circumstances of life. Thus, it is all right that children should become aware that life can be threatening or difficult. Such awareness is psychologically healthy. However, we must help them to see the threats and difficulties of life from the point of view of an unthreatened and spiritually awakened consciousness. We do this by helping them to Realize a breathing, feeling relationship to the Universal Power, the Divine Personality of God.

As parents and adult friends of children you must communicate this Communion with God directly to children all the time. Encourage them to feel it. Then bring them to see how the Enlightened person overcomes difficulties in life. Through stories about such Enlightened beings, our children can discover the Power that really conquers the demons! You cannot look to the TV-and-storybook public world for such morally useful literature. You must seek out literature from the sacred spiritual traditions. In this fellowship you also have the example of my own life and the stories I have written for children. These are the kinds of stories that must be the cultural foundation for the children of devotees, and any other stories must be interpreted from the radical point of view offered by this Teaching.

Children must learn how to live from a spiritual point of view, how to live Ecstatically in the feeling of God. They should be practicing Ecstasy, Happiness. They must understand that Happiness fundamentally is what existence is all about. They must acquire spiritual strength for confronting the limitations of their circumstances, and they should not be permitted to play the threatened neurotic games of not feeling happy and free, and spiritually, emotionally, and physically alive. You must establish them in this positive consciousness. Their worldly associations actually reinforce in them a negative, threatened, mortal consciousness. Thus, their principal occupation must be all the ways of learning, adapting, and enjoying in association with God—not merely with the idea of God or the word "God" but with the Living Reality.

Our children must breathe, feel, and act in relationship to that Living Presence. Otherwise, they will soon acquire many other complex associations, games, and functions. If you have not created in them a fundamentally positive sense of existence, they will adapt to the next stage of life with neurotic complexity, you see. Then what will happen when they become sexually active, for example? Or when they go out to work in the world? They will marry and live an ordinary life. But what will they be if they have not realized a fundamental position that is altogether positive, if they have not realized each level of their adaptation from that positive point of view?

The trouble with ordinary people is that they were never established fundamentally, truly, and altogether in the Transcendental Realization of God. Instead, they adapted to all the patterns of their functions in a weakened, threatened, Narcissistic way, emotionally dissociated from all their intimate relations and ultimately, and fundamentally, from God.

How much of what your children do is actual Ecstatic practice? It is not that you are to learn Ecstasy when you are forty, you see! By not obliging them to this practice we are forcing our children to choose an alternative to Ecstasy. You must be very mindful of this possibility and reinforce in each child what is Ecstatic, self-transcending, and Life-positive. You must give them the freedom and the opportunity to be Ecstatic in their condition.

Children should enjoy a feeling, breathing relationship with the Mystery. They must learn to recognize the Happiness that is felt in relationship to the Mystery. Childhood should be seen in terms of a pattern of growth where the child is always served to transcend the limits of his or her current adaptation, through living association with the spiritual principle of Happiness. Get children to do something different than the usual life! Orient them to a spiritual understanding and practice of existence.

Establish children in a life-positive consciousness. Occupy them with living, adapting, enjoying, breathing, feeling, and relating to the Mystery or God. We should be helping children to practice Ecstasy. And in the midst of their life of feeling and breathing the Mystery, children need to acquire spiritual strength in relationship to the limits imposed by the body and the world.

There is a fundamental sense of the Living Eternal Principle of Life that will pull children through the very real feeling of being collapsed and threatened. If they have not realized a fundamental position that is positive and transcendental, they will adapt to a weak, threatened relationship to all their functions.

All children develop emotional problems inherently, directly. It is their native fear and threatened disposition that we have to touch and change. They need love, physical contact, God-games,[1] devotional and moral stories. Through your own demonstration, help them to feel, trust, and value relationships. Help them to see how the emotional problem has created a life-negative pattern in every area of life. Parents should very clearly know and feel their children's specific emotional patterns of dramatizing the threatened disposition. This threatened disposition is obviated by strengthening their fundamental sense of the Eternal Life Principle.

Read them "The Secret of How to Change."[2] Every area of their life must be rejuvenated. Help them to hear the Truth to the point of Ecstasy. What we should be helping children to do is practice Ecstasy.

We must give our children the cause and freedom to be Ecstatic. Children must understand what Ecstasy is, what Happiness is. Parents and teachers should discover the functional dimension to which children are sensitive at every stage of adaptation, and then teach

1. "God-games" are playful activities in which children practice feeling-sensitivity to the Mystery or the Divine Presence as an integral part of the play.

2. See chapter 8 for this essay by Da Free John.

them in those functional terms. Adults must be relaxed in their inspection of the qualities of children. They must communicate the Life-positive message, the bodily, emotional, feeling expression of God as Radiant Energy, felt as breathing. They must associate children with the sense of being Energy, of being the Mystery.

Children are involved in a spiritual struggle, working out a spiritual problem. Therefore, all children should be Ecstatic and awake, consorting bodily with the feeling of the Mystery. We must give them the gift of a fundamental emotional disposition of Happiness that is as native to them as feeling and breathing—a spiritual, Happy understanding of the Mystery of life.

Chapter 8

The Secret of How to Change

an essay by Da Free John
October 1978

T rue change and higher human adaptation are not made on the basis of any self-conscious resistance to old, degenerative, and subhuman habits. Change is not a matter of <u>not</u> doing something. It is a matter of doing something <u>else</u>, something that is inherently right, free, and pleasurable. Therefore, the key is insight and the freedom to feel and participate in ways of functioning that are right and new.

The tendencies and patterns of our earlier adaptations are not wrong. They were appropriate enough in their own moment of creation, and there is no need to feel guilt or despair about them. Likewise, efforts to oppose and change them are basically fruitless. Such efforts are forms of conflict, and they only reinforce the modes of self-possession.

What is not used becomes obsolete, whereas what is opposed is kept before us. Therefore, the creative principle of change is the one of relaxed inspection and awareness of existing tendencies and persistent, full feeling orientation to right, new, regenerative functional patterns. If this is done consistently and in ecstatic resort to the Living Divine, free growth is assured.

Have no regrets. Resort to the Divine in Truth and in the present. All that has been done by anyone had its logic in its time. Only God avails. Whatever is your habit in this moment is not wrong. It is simply a beginning. No habit is necessary, but it is only tending to persist, because it has not yet been replaced by further growth. Hear the Teaching of Truth, and understand what is the right, ultimate, and regenerative pattern of each function of Man. Feel free of all negative judgments about what you have done and what you tend to do. Turn with full feeling-attention to the creative affair of new adaptation in most positive Communion with the God who is Life, and who is Alive as all beings.

Chapter 9

Feel the Mystery and You Won't Feel So Bad!

by Peter Churchill

In 1978, several months after I first began teaching the meditation practices from *What to Remember to Be Happy* to the children at Mound Builder Free School, the father of one of the boys told me a story of the effectiveness of these practices. Phil and his six-year-old son Zack were driving to the grocery store to do the week's shopping for their family. On the way, they passed through a busy intersection. Suddenly a large truck careened through the opposite red light on a collision course with their car. Phil hit the brakes and swerved sharply to the right; the truck missed them by a matter of inches.

As their car skidded to a stop, Phil anxiously looked over at Zack to make sure he was not hurt, and asked him if he was okay. In a matter-of-fact tone, Zack said, "I'm okay, but you know, Dad, if you feel the Mystery and breathe it you won't feel so bad!" Phil's humor was immediately restored.

After Phil recounted this story to me, he acknowledged that he had read *What to Remember to Be Happy* with Zack many times. He also confessed that he had not really taken it completely seriously. But after this incident he changed his mind. He saw that the instructions and practices of "feeling and breathing the Mystery" were very real and useful to his son, who had remained unruffled and calm in that critical situation of danger.

Chapter 10

Remember the Mystery
in Which You Live

a conversation with Da Free John
October 28, 1978

CHILD: Master Da, I have a personal discipline not to be righteous. But I'm still righteous a lot, and I can't really find a way to stop it.

MASTER DA FREE JOHN: What do you mean "righteous"?

CHILD: Well, I try to be smart, you know. I do things like telling somebody something, just walking by somebody and saying something to him, not really meaning it, just being rude.

MASTER DA FREE JOHN: Are you angry about something?

CHILD: I'm angry when I say it.

MASTER DA FREE JOHN: What are you angry about?

CHILD: Well, I'm just inside myself.

MASTER DA FREE JOHN: Why do you think you are angry? Do you feel angry a lot?

CHILD: Not too much, but sometimes I feel real angry.

MASTER DA FREE JOHN: Is being righteous a way of being angry?

CHILD: Yes.

MASTER DA FREE JOHN: So?

CHILD. Do you have a way that you can tell me that I can stop being righteous? (Everyone in the room laughs, enjoying the simple honesty of the young boy.)

MASTER DA FREE JOHN: Yes. If you love. If you will love people and persist in that feeling, allow yourself to love people all the time, then you will not be righteous in the way that you are talking about. It is fine every now and then to tell somebody where he (or she) is at. (Laughter.) You have to be able to know the difference between behavior in people that is all right and behavior that is not all right, that is negative. But if you love them, then you will know the difference between the things they do that are good and the things that are not. And you will be able to talk to them about the things that are not good without being righteous, without being angry, you see. You will be able to be Happy with them, because you will know at that moment that you also love them. Whereas when you are being righteous, you are not aware of the fact that you love them. You forget about that for a minute.

You have to learn about this loving feeling. Whenever we do not love, whenever we do not feel in this world, we start getting angry. And after we have been angry for a long time, we start getting afraid. We start to feel bad. So, we have to learn how to be able to love all the time, how to feel all the time. We have to be able to feel the world. A lady who was just talking to me said she gets up in the morning unhappy about the fact that the world exists. Well, the mood that she was in at that moment is not the mood of a devotee. A devotee wakes up and, even though things may not be going too well, he feels God. He knows God is all over this world, all inside the world, you see, inside everyone and outside everyone. He feels that the world is about God, that the world is about Love. But people on television and people who are not being Happy do not know that the world is about God.

They do not know that the world is about Love. That is why they do not love very much. That is why they are always talking about themselves and about negative things.

So, if you are angry and righteous, it is just that you have forgotten for a moment that the world is about God, and that the world is about Love, and that you are about Love. And there is nothing you can do about being righteous if you forget to love, if you forget that the world is about God. You cannot stop being righteous by trying not to be righteous. You will stop being righteous when you forget about being righteous, which means you have to remember to love. *What to Remember to Be Happy*—I have written a book on the subject.

You are all the time remembering what you have to remember to be angry and righteous. Instead, you have to remember what you have to remember in order to be Happy, and that means you have to remember God. You have to remember the Mystery in which you live. You have to remember to love, and you have to love, and you have to practice loving people. Do not wait for it to just happen. You have to practice loving people. And you have to communicate love to them. You have to say you love them. You have to do things for them that are full of the feeling of love for them. You see? So, find out what you have to remember to be Happy and do that. If you do that, then you will forget to be angry and righteous.

And sometimes you may have something to say to somebody about something that he (or she) is doing that is not very good, but it will not be the same as righteousness. You will tell this to him because you love him. And when you tell him, you will even sound like you love him. There are even bad people here and there. You probably have not met any really bad people lately, not any really bad ones. But even the really bad ones are alive in the same world. They are with God just like you. They have some things to learn, but you cannot teach them without loving them. You cannot teach anybody anything without being Happy with them. And you cannot be Happy with anybody else unless you are Happy. You cannot always wait for others to do something to make you Happy, you see. You have to be Happy, and then you make other people Happy too.

116

Chapter 11

Pandas, Woodpeckers, and Renunciation

by William Tsiknas
March 21, 1983

The children living in Hermitage are sources of joy for everyone, as is the Master's Teaching Play with them. The following conversation between Master Da and three brahmacharya students reveals his genius in adapting his Teaching on Radical Transcendentalism to seven-year-olds.

Master Da asked one girl, "What is it that you really like?"

She thought for a moment and then answered, "Pandas!"

Master Da said, "What if you had an infinite number of pandas, as many as you wanted—would that make you happy?"

"Yes!" said the girl, smiling a big smile.

"But what if you could only have pandas," said Master Da. "Nothing else! No people, no toys, no books, nothing else around you except pandas."

She began shaking her head and firmly changed her answer to no.

Master Da then asked, "Well, what would it be that you could have, and have nothing else at all forever but only that one thing, that would make you happy?"

The girl looked at the Master quietly for a time and then she said, "You."

"You mean me—this body here?" asked Master Da.

"No," she said, "my Spiritual Master."

"Who is that?" the Master asked. "Do you mean Happiness?"

"Yes," replied the girl.

"Well," said Master Da, "how do you get That?"

She became confused. "I don't know," she said.

The Master raised his eyebrows. "You don't know?" he demanded. "I thought you were supposed to be a practitioner!"

"I am a practitioner," said the girl.

"Where is the Happiness then?" asked Master Da.

She touched her heart and said, "Right here!"

"That's right," said the Master. "And when you feel That Happiness, you forget about everything else." He opened his arms to the room. "You forget about all of this." He slapped his knee. "You even forget about the body. That's the Big Place—the Happiness Place. And it's very Big! You don't need anything else when you are There. You don't need toys, or books, or TV, or sweets. You don't even need a panda!" Master Da looked around at all the children. "Or a polar! Or a Woody Woodpecker! Or an E.T.!" he said, listing their favorite stuffed toys. He smiled at the girl. "There are no pandas in the Happiness Place."

The Master continued, "What we are doing here in Hermitage is finding out that you can be Happy without having or doing a lot of things. All the grown-ups here have already left behind a lot of the things they had before. And the longer we stay here, the more things we will stop having and doing. That is what it is to be a renunciate."

Master Da then asked, "What about all the people back on the mainland?[1] Why are they still having and doing all those things?"

Another girl spoke up. "They probably think they need those things to be Happy."

"Yes!" said Master Da. "A lot of grown-ups are in trouble because of thinking they are un-Happy and thinking that they need things to

---

1. Master Da Free John and the Hermitage Renunciate Order were on an island in the Pacific while the search for a permanent Hermitage site was in progress. His reference is to practitioners on several continents around the world.

make them Happy. They have the 'I-gotta-getties' and the 'I-need-it-nowies.' But these people are only <u>thinking</u> they are un-Happy. So, what you must do is realize that you are only <u>thinking</u> you are un-Happy. And instead of doing that, just remember that before you started thinking you were un-Happy, you are already Happy. Already!" said Master Da loudly. Then he looked around at all the <u>children</u>.

"You can feel that right now, can't you? That you are already Happy?"

"Yes!" they said.

"Well, then," said Master Da with a smile, "<u>that</u> is the practice!"

Chapter 12

Look at the Sunlight on the Water

by Peter Churchill

M aster Da Free John once invited some children to an occasion at a swimming beach. At the beach, he chose a spot overlooking a wide expanse of water, and sat down on the sand. Perhaps you remember what you learned to do at the beach when you were a child—leap around in the sand, dig holes, and chase in and out of the water. On this occasion, the children present did just that. Master Da sat quietly, simply Radiating Happiness.

At first, in their excitement, the children were insensitive to their environment and to Master Da. They were just running, playing, laughing, yelling, doing what they had previously learned at the beach. Master Da watched their play for a while, and then called them over and said, "Sit down, be quiet, and look at the sunlight on the water. Can't you feel the Divine Mystery?" The children, considering his question, sat down on the sand with him. They contemplated the great sheet of water and gazed at the brilliant patterns of sunlight reflected on the waves. One by one they each began to practice the exercises they had learned in *What to Remember to Be Happy*. Soon each child felt the tangible Presence of the Divine Mystery pervading the color and life and movement of the ocean. After sitting for a time with Master Da, they returned calmly and happily to their play, restored to a natural equanimity of body and mind. Their lesson in conscious discipline had been learned.

Appendix

The Seven Stages of Life

THE FIRST THREE STAGES OF LIFE

Heart-Master Da has described the physical, emotional, mental, psychic, Spiritual, Transcendental, and Divine development of the human individual in terms of seven stages. His model of the seven stages of life is a complete description of human and superhuman evolution, and it therefore gives an overview of the essential lessons and Realizations in the Way of the Heart. Beyond that, Heart-Master Da's Teaching-Revelation of the seven stages of life is a great Gift to practitioners of all schools, because it is a comprehensive, unifying framework for understanding the apparently infinite variety of religious and Spiritual practices and philosophies and for relating them to one another and to ultimate Realization. It also clarifies the significance of the various aspects of an Adept's life and Teaching, and it provides a clear standard by which to understand the various experiences and Realizations of Spiritual life. Heart-Master Da's Wisdom-Teaching on the seven stages of life is therefore one of the most useful Revelations He has Given to people who are interested in considering the Truth.

The first stage of life, which occupies the years from conception and birth to approximately age seven, is a process of individuation, or identification with the personal physical body in the waking state, in which the human being gradually adapts functionally to physical existence and achieves physical, mental, emotional, psychic, and psychological independence from the mother and from all others. The mature individual in the first stage of life is not isolated, but he or she has begun to be consciously related to others and the world of Nature. The signs of maturity in the first stage of life and the movement toward the second stage of life generally begin at age five or six. No sudden transition marks the distinction between the first and second stages of life (or, in general, between consecutive stages of the first six stages of life), but instead the individual shows growing evidence of this transition, until he or she is more or less wholly occupied with the interests of the second stage of life.

The second stage of life is a process of socialization, or social exploration and growth in relationships, first on an intimate scale and then in an ever larger social sphere as the individual becomes attentive to social visibility and acceptance by others. Though genital sexuality is not properly the sphere of the second stage of life, the individual does develop a significant, though partial, sexual self-identity at this time. But primarily the individual becomes emotionally sensitive to self, others, and the natural world, including the energy fields that surround and permeate them, and maturity in the second stage of life is indicated by the development of true "morality" (or the social orientation of relational love), based on feeling-sensitivity to self, others, and Nature. The most obvious sign of the transition to the third stage of life is puberty. Entrance into the third stage of life generally takes place between ages twelve and fourteen, though the progressive evidence of movement toward the third stage of life may begin as early as age ten.

The third stage of life, which is a process of integration and self-presentation as a fully differentiated and defined sexual and social character, involves the development and application of discriminative intelligence and the will. The individual who has adapted to the third stage of life shows signs of full preparation (physically, emotionally, etherically, psychically, and mentally) to enter into the social, personal, and Spiritual responsibilities of a truly human adult. This requires the ability to be present as a free and intelligent will and as love under all conditions. While many societies, particularly in the West, consider an individual to be an adult generally around age eighteen, full preparation for adulthood, including advanced education and development of occupational skills, typically continues into the mid-twenties, and the process of integration continues to mature even throughout life.

The stages of life beyond the first three are not associated with any typical ranges of age, and the rate of growth in the higher stages of life varies with each individual. Even so, because (at this moment in human history) most people only partially, or imperfectly, adapt to the requirements of the first three stages of life (and do not otherwise discover either the personal motive or the cultural opportunity for growth beyond the context of the first three stages of life), most people in this era do not (and will not) develop beyond the third stage of life (unless new personal and cultural factors intervene to stimulate and nurture such growth).

In the first stage of life, people generally reactively misadapt to individuation as separation and separativeness, and they are thus unable to resolve (by relinquishment or even acceptance) their dependence on others, especially the mother. This leads to a sense of dissociation from the Ultimate Source of Love and Nurturing and to a sense of doubt about those on whom one depends for love and support. Thus, people typically adapt un-Happily to socialization in the second stage of life through doubt of self and doubt of love in others, which lead to the feeling of being rejected and the need to reject others, punishing them for assumed un-love. As a result, the struggle to achieve integration in the third stage of life becomes the futile drama of protracted adolescence, or the never-resolved conflict between childish dependence and rebellious and destructive independence. Because full human maturity is not achieved, and because society fails to rightly communicate the approach of the fourth stage of life, most people spend their entire life within the limitations of the first three stages of life, rather than grow beyond them through higher adaptation and self-transcendence.

THE FOURTH, FIFTH, AND SIXTH STAGES OF LIFE

Heart-Master Da has spoken of the significance of the transition to the fourth stage of life:

HEART-MASTER DA: The great transition that must be realized is the transition from the first three stages of life to the fourth. To be truly established in the fourth stage of life is the great accomplishment toward which you are moving, or should be moved. To be established in the fourth stage of life and receive Grace directly through Blessing is to be established in Divine Communion, the freedom of God-Realization by Grace.

You must grow into that fourth stage realization. You must grow beyond self-contraction, the social personality, the first three stages of life. That is your calling and the calling to mankind in general. The practice in the context of stages of life beyond that is something you can do if the evidence that makes it impossible to do other than practice in the context of those higher stages is shown by Grace.[1]

The fourth stage of life is thus an important turning point, when the individual begins to move fully into the Spiritual dimension beyond the functional and relational concerns that characterize the first three stages and to develop the subtle, non-physical dimensions of the body-mind. It is in the fourth stage of life that the heart awakens to That which transcends merely human interests, and the individual begins to practice religion in its true (or fullest) sense. The individual becomes capable of heart-felt surrender to the "Merely Present" Divine Person and Condition (or the Reality, Self, and Self-Radiant Form of all beings and things), and he or she Realizes intimacy with the Divine Person and Condition via reception of the Living Spirit-Current. The fourth stage process of Spiritualization through self-transcending devotional Communion with the Divine Person is expressed internally through heart-feeling and meditation, and it is expressed externally through constant service to the Divine in all relations and circumstances.

Maturity in the fourth stage of life is indicated by equanimity of the frontal personality (or the personality of the waking state), fullness in the "frontal line" (or the gross physical and etheric dimensions of the body-mind), and the movement of the Spirit-Current during meditation from descent in the frontal line to ascent in the "spinal line" (or the subtle dimension of the body-mind) to the degree of steady concentration at the "Ajna Door" (or the "third eye", the subtle psychic center between and behind the eyebrows and associated with the brain core).

Meditation in the fifth stage of life is primarily a process of transforming and transcending the mind through absorptive Communion with the Divine Person as the All-Pervading Spirit-Current, and the fifth stage practitioner may observe and transcend the subtle and mystical dimensions of the body-mind and their corresponding cosmic planes. The Spiritual practice of mystical ascent in the fifth

1. From a talk by Heart-Master Da, July 20, 1986, published in *The Laughing Man,* vol. 6, no. 4, p. 33.

stage of life focuses at and above the "Ajna Door", via concentration in internal sensations, such as inner lights and sounds, which are stimulated as attention rises in the Spirit-Current. The internal mystical and Spiritual phenomena encountered at this stage are forms of "Savikalpa Samadhi" (literally, "ecstasy with form"), and the highest form of Savikalpa Samadhi is "Cosmic Consciousness", in which subtle or even bodily awareness remains, but Consciousness otherwise perceives all existence as an Infinite Unity. The fifth stage of life may culminate in the Realization of formless ecstasy (or "conditional Nirvikalpa Samadhi"), in which attention stands free of body and mind as it temporarily merges in the Divine Light felt to be infinitely above the crown of the head, but in any case the fifth stage of life must culminate in an Awakening that produces an equivalent effect in the re-orientation of attention beyond body, mind, and conditional experience.

The sixth stage of life represents another major turning point in the Spiritual Process. Whereas Spiritual practice in the first five stages is occupied with the transcendence of the self-contraction in the context of conditional existence, the sixth stage of life marks the beginning of the direct transcendence of attention, which is the root of the self-contraction and conditional existence, through devotional absorption in the Divine Person as the Transcendental Self, or Consciousness Itself. The sixth stage of life, which begins with stable Realization of the Position of the "Witness-Consciousness" (or the mere "Witness" of the objects of attention) prior to body and mind, is mature when the Witnessing self Awakens to its real Condition as Transcendental Consciousness, or the Very Self, and the sixth stage of life may ultimately culminate in "Jnana Samadhi", or absorption in the Transcendental (and inherently Spiritual) Self-Position, or Consciousness Itself, exclusive of all conditional objects and states.

The fourth, fifth, and sixth stages of life are each associated with a characteristic error or misadaptation, the sign of egoic seeking. The fourth stage error is to treat the self as an eternally separate entity dependent upon a Divine Other Who (or Whose favor) is to be sought unendingly. The fifth stage error is to seek or otherwise cling to all the countless phenomena of mystical introversion and the "Visions" of the One Mind (in Savikalpa Samadhi), or to the temporary Bliss of psychic dissolution (in conditional Nirvikalpa Samadhi), feeling that these are necessary for Happiness, or that they are Truth Itself. The sixth stage error is the tendency to hold on to the Subjective Position of Conciousness, as if the Realization of Divine Consciousness depends upon strategically excluding Consciousness from Its objects and thus cutting off all awareness of objective conditional phenomena. Without true understanding of these errors, the experiential phenomena of the first five stages of life are binding and ego-reinforcing distractions that only delay the course of Realization, and the Self-Realization of the sixth stage of life remains a temporary and effortful achievement.

THE SEVENTH STAGE OF LIFE

The Enlightened individual in the seventh stage of life has (in the "Perfect" fulfillment, or transcendence, of the sixth stage of life) Realized "Perfect" Devotion, or constant, inherent, uncaused, and unconditional Identification with the Self-Radiant and Self-Existing Divine Person and Condition. Through Self-Abiding in the Divine Condition, conditional existence and all its objects are "Recognized" to be merely unnecessary and non-binding modifications of Self-Radiant Consciousness, and in that case, no matter what arises, no limited self arises. Therefore, the God-Realized individual remains absorbed in the Love-Bliss of Consciousness Itself, even in the midst of arising conditions. Such is "Sahaj Samadhi", the "inherent" or "natural" Condition of "Open-Eyed" God-Realization. And when the Self-Radiance of Consciousness Shines so "Brightly" that no conditions are even noticed, the Enlightened individual is absorbed in Love-Bliss beyond all knowing. Heart-Master Da calls this "Bhava Samadhi", and the ultimate form of Bhava Samadhi is the permanent "Outshining" of conditional existence, or "Translation" into the "Divine Self-Domain".

Heart-Master Da has commented that the seventh stage of life fulfills the primary motives that are active in all of the earlier stages:

HEART-MASTER DA: The motive of the sixth stage of life is the transcendence of the conditional self in the Transcendental Self. That transcendence is the very principle of the seventh stage of life. The purpose of the fifth stage of life is to transcend conditional self, mind, and the body in the very Current or Spiritual Reality in Which it appears, in Which it is arising. This is Realized in the seventh stage of life in the Awakening of Consciousness and Its Divine Recognition of phenomena. The fourth stage of life is devotion of self to its transcendence, in other words to its Source. That devotion is fulfilled in Transcendental Self-Realization. The purpose of the first three stages of life, or of conditional existence itself, apart from association with the organization of human personality and the adaptation to functional systems, is Happiness, which is only tasted occasionally through contact with conditions.

But with the Awakening of Transcendental Self-Realization it becomes clear that this Happiness is Inherent. It is the very Nature of existence. As soon as contraction, or conditional existence, is assumed, a limitation is placed on Happiness, and It is given only that conditional opportunity to reveal Itself. What if no conditions are placed on It? Then, It is constant, inherently Realized. And once It is Realized, all conditions rush out of the heart like birds released from a snare, are seen, Recognized, and transcended to the point of "Outshining", as if they were flying into the sun. (March 16, 1986)

Heart-Master Da's Call has always been to the direct Realization of the Divine in the seventh stage. And the priorly Free and Happy disposition of the seventh stage of life is the fundamental intuition that informs practice in the Way of the Heart, even from the beginning. The conventional view of Spiritual life can be characterized as a "path of return" that leads progressively through the seven stages of life, assuming the problems and limitations of each stage, while working toward the fulfillment (and, perhaps, eventual transcendence) of that stage. However, the seven stages of life are not rightly viewed as a progression of possible experiences, but they are a school of essential lessons, each of which, when rightly understood, points beyond itself to the Ultimate Realization.

While the great path of return may require countless lifetimes, the Way of Satsang offered by the True Heart-Master may lead anyone in a single lifetime directly to transcend each and all of the stages of life, through heartfelt Communion with the Divine Person contacted in the Mere and Blessing Presence of the True Heart-Master.

THE PRINCIPLE OF RETREAT

The Culture of Practice in The Free Daist Communion

THE PRINCIPLE OF RETREAT

Traditionally, when an individual wished to intensify the practice of Spiritual life, he or she entered into a circumstance of retreat, renouncing for a time those activities and habits that might tend to draw energy and attention away from the Spiritual Process. Living in a quiet and secluded environment and adopting a simplified mode of living, the individual concentrated all his or her energy and attention on Spiritual practice and Spiritual and Transcendental Divine Realization. This "Principle of Retreat" is also the foundation of practice in The Free Daist Communion.

Heart-Master Da has summarized the foundation of the Way of the Heart as the two-armed "Principle of Retreat", comprising the supportive "discipline of the body-mind", or "Sila",[1] and the primary "discipline of attention", or "Understanding". This basic Principle of Retreat is ultimately practiced in the Spiritually Transmitted Mere and Blessing Presence of the True Heart-Master, but it is also the active Principle of the process that is engaged even when one first studies Heart-Master Da's Teaching Word or attends a public presentation. (At an introductory lecture, for instance, the discipline of the body-mind is effective, in that one must at least sit in one spot for an hour or two, participating bodily in the occasion of the presentation. The discipline of attention is fulfilled by directing awareness to the consideration at hand. Thus, one forgoes other possible distractions and attractions and devotes oneself, body and mind, to pondering the Teaching Argument.)

When one becomes a full beginning practitioner of the Way of the Heart (at practicing stage one, following the initial period of intensive student-consideration of the Way of the Heart), a comprehensive

---

1. "Sila" is a Pali Buddhist term meaning "habit, behavior, conduct". It connotes the disposition of equanimity wherein energy and attention are free for the Spiritual Process.

discipline of the body-mind is developed via the free and intentional practice of positively useful and personally appropriate life-conditions (or functional, practical, and relational disciplines in the areas of diet and health, exercise, sexuality, service, cooperative community, and the like). These disciplines act to quicken the process of self-observation by reflecting the self-contraction in every context of daily life, and they also progressively (or eventually) free energy and attention for the Spiritual Process. As one's practice of the Way matures, self-discipline naturally and inevitably takes the form of the minimization of all possible distractions from the Spiritual Process and the magnification of the disposition of true equanimity and real self-surrender. Ultimately, the discipline of the body-mind is fulfilled in Spiritual and Transcendental Divine Self-Realization, or utter, continuous, and eternal freedom from identification with bodily and mental limits.

The discipline of attention, the other arm of the Principle of Retreat, first develops, through study, into real pondering of the Wisdom-Teaching as it applies to the conditions of one's daily life. As one's practice of the Way strengthens, pondering naturally and progressively evolves into the capacity for real meditation. And meditation is ultimately fulfilled in the transcendence of attention altogether in continuous Spiritual and Transcendental Divine Self-Realization in the seventh stage of life.

For devotees (at practicing stage two, and beyond, through practicing stage seven), the basis of the Way of the Heart is "Satsang" (literally meaning "the Company of Truth"), or the Spiritual relationship between the True Heart-Master and His devotee. Through Spiritual Initiation (or Spiritual Awakening in the Mere and Blessing Presence of the True Heart-Master, and via the Spirit-Baptism received from the True Heart-Master), the devotee learns to contact the Spiritual, Transcendental, and Divine Person (or Reality) from moment to moment. Therefore, the True Heart-Master's Transmission (or Mere and Blessing Presence) is the primary Means for the devotee's ultimate Awakening.

For the practicing devotee, both arms of the Principle of Retreat are founded in Satsang, or the Spiritual relationship to the True Heart-Master. Without Heart-Master Da's Transforming Influence (or Mere and Blessing Presence), all "disciplines" are no more than empty ritual and all "understanding" is an illusion of the body-mind, but when they are practiced in right devotional (or Spiritual) relationship to the True Heart-Master, the disciplines of the body-mind and attention become effective means of submission to Mastery by the Graceful Accomplishing Power of the Divine Person.

Now Heart-Master Da has Retired from His Teaching Work. He resides at Translation Island Hermitage Sanctuary, where He lives rather privately, served and cared for by a small number of individual practitioners from around the world. Personal access to Him at the Hermitage Sanctuary is generally limited to residents of the Hermitage, practicing devotees (when such devotees appear) on meditation retreat, individual practitioners on special service retreat, and other (occasional) visiting representatives from the total worldwide gathering of practitioners of the Way of the Heart. Such access, if and when it occurs, is generally limited to formal occasions of service, discussions about the Way, and, for devotees, occasions of meditation or Darshan (Spiritual sighting of the True Heart-Master). And in the however rare event of His travel from the Hermitage to other Sanctuaries and to centers of consideration and practice around the world, Heart-Master Da will generally continue to be personally accessible in the same manner as He is in Hermitage.

Even though He is (and has been) entirely free of both institutional and cultural responsibilities, Heart-Master Da will continue to spontaneously Transmit (or Give access to) His Spirit-Baptism and Mere and Blessing Presence. In the future, those who are fully prepared as practicing devotees will likely have the opportunity of occasional appropriate access to Heart-Master Da's personal Company for the purpose of receiving His direct Transmission, but, more and more, as the number of those who have truly received His Baptism increases, and as the number of truly mature and advanced practicing devotees increases, Heart-Master Da's Transmission will be Extended and perpetuated through the Instrumentality of the total Baptized Community of His practicing devotees (as well as through the Agency of Retreat Sanctuaries He has Empowered, or may in the future Empower, for the use of His devotees). This Transmission via the Instrumentality of the Baptized Community will not depend upon elaborate efforts or intentions on the part of Heart-Master Da, but It will take place spontaneously (as It does even in His personal Company), based upon every devotee's active and expressive devotional and Spiritual alignment and receptivity to Heart-Master Da. Over time, this Transmission may be further Implemented through the Instrumentality of devotees who are much advanced in the practice of the Way of the Heart (and the Agency of those Awakened even into the context of the seventh stage of life), but, in any case, this Transmission will continue to Function through the Baptized Community as a whole (or otherwise directly, from or in the Free Heart-Radiance of Heart-Master Da), and without any self-conscious intention on the part of the general members or the cultural leaders of the Baptized Community of devotees. Therefore, in the future, whenever and wherever members of the Baptized Community will gather in right meditative and devotional occasions, Heart-Master Da's Mere and Blessing Presence will be spontaneously magnified for the sake of all. In this manner, the Gifts of the Heart and the Way of the Heart will be perpetuated in all the times and spaces of mankind.

THE FREE DAIST COMMUNION

The Free Daist Communion has the responsibility to communicate and provide the cultural context for the study and practice of the Way that Heart-Master Da has Revealed. The Free Daist Communion derives its present name from Heart-Master Da's Free and Complete Revelation of the Divine Person and the Way of the Heart:

Free—In contrast to the traditional paths of seeking, the Way of the Heart is (from the beginning of real "hearing" and "seeing") founded on the Perfect Freedom that cannot be lost or found, but only Realized, the Freedom that is already our native Condition.

Daist—"Da" is an ancient sacred Name in many traditions, including Hinduism and Buddhism, and it may be translated as "the Giver of Life", or simply the "Giver". The "Daist", or, more properly, "Free Daist", religion (Revealed by Heart-Master Da and founded on the Radical Understanding awakened by His Teaching Word) is (in its fullness) the inherently Free practice of devotion to and Realization of the Divine Person, called Da, the Giver, Who Is Freedom, or always already Free Being, Love-Bliss, and Consciousness Itself.

Communion—The name "Communion" indicates that this gathering (or total community) of people is dedicated to preparing for and practicing Communion with (and Realization of) the eternal Divine Person and Condition, and that we are also dedicated to communicating to all people the opportunity for such Divine Communion and Realization.

Beginners in the Daist religion (or Way) Freely observe themselves and increasingly understand and release the action of self-contraction that is the root of suffering through study and meditative pondering of Heart-Master Da's Teaching Word, which is the Given Agency of self-revelation and self-understanding. And devotee-practitioners of the Daist religion (or Way) Freely worship and surrender to (or Commune with) the Giver (or the Transcendental Divine Reality or Self of all), and they Freely acknowledge the One Who is the Giver in the Mere Presence, the Blessing Work, and the Teaching-Revelation of Heart-Master Da.

The primary purpose of The Free Daist Communion, a tax-exempt, non-profit religious organization, is to serve Heart-Master Da's Work to Awaken individuals directly to the Living Divine Reality. The Communion exists to fulfill four great obligations:

• to care for its Sacred Treasures, which are the True Heart-Master and the principal means of His Agency, namely the Sacred Wisdom-Teaching of Heart-Master Da and the Empowered Sanctuaries

• to disseminate the Wisdom-Teaching of Heart-Master Da and the history or "leelas" of His Work

• to provide educational and cultural services for practitioners, students, lay members, and the general public, and to provide appropriate access to the sacred Instruments and Agencies of the Way of the Heart

• to cultivate an intelligent and discriminative understanding of the Great Tradition of human cultural, religious, mystical, Spiritual, Transcendental, and Divine Wisdom that is mankind's inheritance (especially honoring the contributions of the Adepts) and thereby to counter the modern trends of scientific materialism and religious provincialism

THE SERVICES OF THE FREE DAIST COMMUNION

The Free Daist Communion is the general or inclusive name of the total institutional body of men and women who freely choose to study, practice, and fulfill the Great Way of the Heart. There are seven stages of practice in The Free Daist Communion.

Practice is prepared for by a period of intensive student participation in the educational programs of The Laughing Man Institute, and the first stage of practice also develops in The Laughing Man Institute. The Laughing Man Institute provides presentations, lectures, seminars, courses, and other cultural opportunities to serve the serious understanding (and application) of Heart-Master Da's Liberating Teaching Arguments and the practice of the Way that He has Revealed.

Practicing stages two through seven are divided into four cultural organizations, or Fellowships:

Practicing stages two and three are developed and completed within The Dawn Horse Fellowship, stages four and five within The Ajna Dharma Fellowship, and stage six within The Advaitayana Buddhist Fellowship. The seventh or Enlightened stage of practice is demonstrated within The Crazy Wisdom Fellowship.

All of the Instructions, Initiations, Tests, and Signs of maturity and Realization at each stage of practice have been summarized and described in great detail in the published Teaching Word of Heart-Master Da.

The Regional Centers of
The Laughing Man Institute

If you wish to participate in The Laughing Man Institute programs in your area, please contact the Regional Center nearest you (listed below*) or contact:

The Laughing Man Institute
750 Adrian Way, Suite 111
San Rafael, CA 94903, U.S.A.
(415) 492-9382

NORTHERN CALIFORNIA
740 Adrian Way
San Rafael, CA 94903
(415) 492-0930

Northern California/Western U.S.A. Area Groups
Nevada City, California
Oakland, California
Palo Alto, California
Roseville, California
Rough 'N Ready, California
Sacramento, California
San Francisco, California
Santa Cruz, California
Santa Rosa, California
Stanford, California
Sunnyvale, California
Boulder, Colorado
Denver, Colorado
Longmont, Colorado

SOUTHWEST U.S.A.
616 Santa Monica Blvd., Suite 218
Santa Monica, CA 90401
(213) 393-1953

Southwest U.S.A. Area Groups
Phoenix, Arizona

Tucson, Arizona
Colton, California
Costa Mesa, California
Glendale, California
Los Alamitos, California
Morro Bay, California
Redondo Beach, California
San Diego, California
San Marcos, California
Santa Barbara, California
Santa Monica, California
Sherman Oaks, California
Whittier, California

SOUTH CENTRAL U.S.A.
1808 Westridge Drive
(P.O. Box 5790)
Austin, Texas 78704
(512) 447-6336

South Central U.S.A. Area Groups
New Orleans, Louisiana
Slidell, Louisiana
Albuquerque, New Mexico
Bedford, Texas
Dallas, Texas
Denton, Texas
Garland, Texas
Houston, Texas
Leander, Texas

*This list is current as of January 1988.

NORTHWEST U.S.A.
918 N.E. 64th St.
Seattle, WA 98115
(206) 527-0260

Northwestern U.S.A./Western Canada Area Groups
Calgary (Alberta), Canada
Moncton (New Brunswick), Canada
Surrey (B.C.), Canada
Vancouver (B.C.), Canada
Winnipeg (Manitoba), Canada
Ketchum, Idaho
Eugene, Oregon
Portland, Oregon
Roseburg, Oregon
Ogden, Utah
Roy, Utah

NORTHEAST U.S.A.
P.O. Box 6
Auburndale, MA 02166
(617) 965-9711

Northeastern U.S.A. Area Groups
Amherst, Massachusetts
Brighton, Massachusetts
Cape Cod, Massachusetts
Dalton, Massachusetts
Rockport, Massachusetts
Springfield, Massachusetts
Wellesley, Massachusetts
Yarmouthsport, Massachusetts
Swedesboro, New Jersey
West Orange, New Jersey
Batavia, New York
Hudson Falls, New York
Islip, New York
Kew Gardens, New York
Mt. Kisco, New York
Bethlehem, Pennsylvania
Philadelphia, Pennsylvania
Richmond, Vermont

MIDWEST U.S.A.
802 Reba Place
Evanston, Illinois 60202
(312) 864-2800

Midwestern U.S.A. Area Groups
Chicago, Illinois
Urbana, Illinois
Western Springs, Illinois
Whitehall, Illinois
New Albany, Indiana
Iowa City, Iowa
Ann Arbor, Michigan
Charlevoix, Michigan
Grand Rapids, Michigan
Southfield, Michigan
Zimmerman, Minnesota
Maryland Heights, Missouri
St. Louis, Missouri
Chesterland, Ohio
Cincinatti, Ohio
Cleveland, Ohio
Columbus, Ohio
Grove City, Ohio
Hartville, Ohio
Kettering, Ohio
Madison, Wisconsin

SOUTHEAST U.S.A.
6516 Western Ave.
Chevy Chase, Maryland 20815
(301) 656-6867

Southeastern U.S.A. Area Groups
Key West, Florida
Miami, Florida
St. Petersburg, Florida
Atlanta, Georgia
Lexington, Kentucky
Mt. Vernon, Kentucky
Baltimore, Maryland
Gaithersburg, Maryland
Chapel Hills, North Carolina
Pineville, North Carolina

Raleigh, North Carolina
Spartanburg, South Carolina
Richmond, Virginia

EASTERN CANADA
88 Owen Blvd.
Willowdale, Ontario M2P 1G3
Canada
(416) 733-1822

Eastern Canada Area Groups
Montreal (Quebec), Canada
Ottawa (Ontario), Canada

THE UNITED KINGDOM AND IRELAND
28 A Poland Street
London W1V 3DB
England
441-734-4217

The United Kingdom and Ireland Area Groups
Cambridge, England
Cheltenham, England
Devon, England
Leeds, England
Manchester, England
Norwich, England
Suffolk, England
Dublin, Ireland
Belfast, N. Ireland

THE NETHERLANDS
Prinsengracht 719
1017JW Amsterdam
The Netherlands
31-20-277-600

The Netherlands/Germany Area Groups
Den Haag, The Netherlands
Haarlem, The Netherlands
Utrecht, The Netherlands
Hamburg, West Germany
West Berlin, West Germany

NEW ZEALAND
21 High Street
CPO Box 3185
Auckland 1
New Zealand
649-774-495

New Zealand Area Groups
Christchurch, New Zealand
Wellington, New Zealand

AUSTRALIA—MELBOURNE
37 Little Collins St.
Melbourne, Victoria 3000
Australia
03-882-8122

Australia—Melbourne Associated Area Groups
Adelaide, South Australia
Prospect, South Australia
Mossman Park, Western Australia
Perth, Western Australia

AUSTRALIA—SYDNEY
265 Elizabeth St.
Sydney, New South Wales 2000
Australia
02-264-5756

Sydney Associated Area Groups
Byron Bay, New South Wales

HAWAII, MEXICO and HONG KONG Area Groups
(For information on these groups, contact The Laughing Man Institute, 750 Adrian Way, San Rafael, CA 94903 U.S.A., or phone [415] 492-9382.)

Hana, Hawaii
Honolulu, Hawaii
Kihei, Hawaii
Lihue, Hawaii
Chiapas, Mexico

The Written and Spoken Teaching Word
of Heart-Master Da

THE SOURCE LITERATURE

These Source Books are the epitome of Heart-Master Da's Wisdom-Teaching on the Attributes, the Secrets, and the Realization of the Heart, or Spiritual, Transcendental, and Divine Consciousness.

THE DAWN HORSE TESTAMENT
Of Heart-Master Da (The Avadhoota Da Love-Ananda Hridayam, Whose Teaching Name Is Da Free John)
$45.00 cloth, $24.95 paper, 801 pages.

THE KNEE OF LISTENING
The Early Life and Radical Spiritual Teachings of Heart-Master Da Love-Ananda (Da Free John)
$10.95 paper, 271 pages.

THE METHOD OF THE SIDDHAS
Talks with Heart-Master Da Love-Ananda (Avadhoota Da Free John) on the Spiritual Technique of the Saviors of Mankind
$14.95 paper, 410 pages.

LOVE-ANANDA GITA
The Free-Song of Love-Bliss
$19.95 cloth, 304 pages.

THE ILLUSION OF RELATEDNESS
Essays on True and Free Renunciation and the Radical Transcendence of Conditional Existence
Third Edition, Revised and Enlarged (New Standard Edition)
$14.95 paper, 168 pages.

THE PRACTICAL TEXTS

The following practical texts elaborate the basic life-disciplines practiced in the Way of the Heart.

THE EATING GORILLA COMES IN PEACE
The Transcendental Principle of Life Applied to Diet and the Regenerative Discipline of True Health
$16.95 paper, 565 pages.

CONSCIOUS EXERCISE AND THE TRANSCENDENTAL SUN
The principle of love applied to exercise and the method of common physical action. A science of whole body wisdom, or true emotion, intended most especially for those engaged in religious or spiritual life.
$12.95 paper, 300 pages.

LOVE OF THE TWO-ARMED FORM
The Free and Regenerative Function of Sexuality in Ordinary Life, and the Transcendence of Sexuality in True Religious or Spiritual Practice
$17.95 paper, 498 pages.

MANUALS OF PRACTICE

The manuals of practice are listed below according to the stages of the development of the Way of the Heart Revealed by Heart-Master Da. The Way of the Heart begins with "listening" to the message of the Teaching Word until true "hearing" or most fundamental self-understanding Awakens. Then "seeing", emotional conversion, or love of the Divine Person and Presence, follows. On the basis of "hearing" and "seeing", true "practice" of the Way of the Heart begins. The manuals of practice can usefully be studied not only by practitioners but by anyone interested in the Way of the Heart.

LISTENING to the Argument of Truth

These books serve the concentrated study and pondering of Heart-Master Da's Fundamental Questions and Teaching Arguments relative to "Narcissus" (or the self-contraction), "Radical Understanding" (or direct feeling-transcendence of the self-contraction), and "Divine Ignorance" (or intuition of Radiant Transcendental Divine Consciousness), all of which Awaken and clarify the motive toward self-transcending Realization of the Divine Person and Presence.

THE HOLY JUMPING-OFF PLACE
An Introduction to the Way of the Heart Revealed by Heart-Master Da Love-Ananda (Avadhoota Da Free John)
Second Edition, Revised and Expanded
$6.95 paper, 192 pages.

THE FOUR FUNDAMENTAL QUESTIONS
Talks and essays about human experience and the actual practice of an Enlightened Way of Life
$4.95 paper, 118 pages.

SCIENTIFIC PROOF OF THE EXISTENCE OF GOD WILL SOON BE
ANNOUNCED BY THE WHITE HOUSE!
*Prophetic Wisdom about the Myths and Idols of mass culture and popular
religious cultism, the new priesthood of scientific and political materialism,
and the secrets of Enlightenment hidden in the body of Man*
$19.95 paper, 430 pages.

DO YOU KNOW WHAT ANYTHING IS?
Talks and Essays on Divine Ignorance
$12.95 paper, 160 pages.

THE ADEPT
*Selections from Talks and Essays by Da Free John [Heart-Master Da] on the
Nature and Function of the Enlightened Teacher*
$12.95 paper, 112 pages.

THE GOD IN EVERY BODY BOOK
Talks and Essays on God-Realization
$5.95 paper, 188 pages.

THE TRANSMISSION OF DOUBT
*Talks and Essays on the Transcendence of Scientific Materialism through
Radical Understanding*
$17.95 paper, 450 pages.

ENLIGHTENMENT AND THE TRANSFORMATION OF MAN
*Selections from Talks and Essays on the Spiritual Process and
God-Realization*
$7.95 paper, 180 pages.

THE YOGA OF CONSIDERATION
AND THE WAY THAT I TEACH
*Talks and Essays on the distinction between preliminary practices and the
radical Way of prior Enlightenment*
$7.95 paper, 100 pages.

THE TRANSCENDENCE OF EGO AND EGOIC SOCIETY (booklet)
$2.00, 20 pages.

SCIENCE, SACRED CULTURE, AND REALITY (booklet)
$2.50, 36 pages.

HEARING and Understanding the Truth

Heart-Master Da has made clear that before true practice of the Way of
the Heart can begin, "hearing" must fundamentally penetrate the activity of
self-contraction and unlock the heart.

THE DREADED GOM-BOO, OR THE IMAGINARY DISEASE THAT RELIGION SEEKS TO CURE
A Collection of Essays and Talks on the "Direct" Process of Enlightenment
$17.95 paper, 430 pages.

THE WAY THAT I TEACH
Talks on the Intuition of Eternal Life
$24.95 cloth, $14.95 paper, 261 pages.

THE BODILY SACRIFICE OF ATTENTION
Introductory Talks on Radical Understanding and the Life of Divine Ignorance
$10.95 paper, 148 pages.

WHAT IS THE CONSCIOUS PROCESS?
Talks and essays on the tacit intuition of Transcendental Consciousness, being a summary consideration of the Way of Radical Understanding or Divine Ignorance
$8.95 paper, 96 pages.

SEEING and the Process of Spiritual Baptism

Real practice of the Way of the Heart is founded on "seeing", or Spirit-Baptism, which is the process of emotional conversion to and Communion with the Spiritual Presence of the Divine Person. Seeing is principally initiated and developed through "Ishta-Guru-Bhakti Yoga", or the esoteric process of devotional acknowledgement of and native identification with the Spiritual and Transcendental Divine Self, Which is Revealed in the Mere and Blessing Presence of the True Heart-Master.

BODILY WORSHIP OF THE LIVING GOD
The Esoteric Practice of Prayer Taught by Da Free John [Heart-Master Da]
$10.95 paper, 194 pages.

COMPULSORY DANCING
Talks and Essays on the spiritual and evolutionary necessity of emotional surrender to the Life-Principle
$5.95 paper, 180 pages.

THE FIRE GOSPEL
Essays and Talks on Spiritual Baptism
$14.95 paper, 224 pages.

"I" IS THE BODY OF LIFE
Talks and Essays on the Art and Science of Equanimity and the Self-Transcending Process of Radical Understanding
$12.95 paper, 180 pages.

PRACTICE and Realization of the Way of the Heart

The manuals listed below describe the mature practice of the Way of the Heart that begins once the foundations of "hearing" and "seeing" are stable. With the Source Texts, these books comprise Heart-Master Da's published instructions on the practice and fulfillment of the Way of the Heart.

THE HYMN OF THE MASTER
A Confessional Recitation on the Mystery of the Spiritual Master based on the principal verses of the Guru Gita (freely selected, rendered, and adapted by Da Free John [Heart-Master Da])
$12.95 paper, 106 pages.

THE BODILY LOCATION OF HAPPINESS
On the Incarnation of the Divine Person and the Transmission of Love-Bliss
$14.95 paper, 262 pages.

THE ENLIGHTENMENT OF THE WHOLE BODY
A Rational and New Prophetic Revelation of the Truth of Religion, Esoteric Spirituality, and the Divine Destiny of Man
$24.95 paper, 600 pages.

THE PARADOX OF INSTRUCTION
An Introduction to the Esoteric Spiritual Teaching of Bubba Free John [Heart-Master Da]
$14.95 paper, 328 pages.

NIRVANASARA
Radical Transcendentalism and the Introduction of Advaitayana Buddhism
$14.95 paper, 262 pages.

THE LIBERATOR (ELEUTHERIOS)
$19.95 cloth, $10.95 paper, 114 pages.

EASY DEATH
Talks and Essays on the Inherent and Ultimate Transcendence of Death and Everything Else
$12.95 paper, 406 pages.

FOR AND ABOUT CHILDREN

WHAT TO REMEMBER TO BE HAPPY
A Spiritual Way of Life for Your First Fourteen Years or So
$5.95 paper, 48 pages.

I AM HAPPINESS
A Rendering for Children of the Spiritual Adventure of Master Da Free John
[Heart-Master Da]
Adapted by Daji Bodha and Lynne Closser from The Knee of Listening *by*
Master Da Free John [Heart-Master Da]
$8.95 paper, 60 pages.

LOOK AT THE SUNLIGHT ON THE WATER
Educating Children for a Life of Self-Transcending Love and Happiness
$10.95 paper, 160 pages.

INSPIRATIONAL AND DEVOTIONAL TEXTS

CRAZY DA MUST SING, INCLINED TO HIS WEAKER SIDE
Confessional Poems of Liberation and Love by the "Western" Adept, Da
Free John [Heart-Master Da]
$12.95 paper, 124 pages.

FOREHEAD, BREATH, AND SMILE
An Anthology of Devotional Readings from the Spiritual Teaching of
Master Da Free John [Heart-Master Da]
$29.95 cloth, 112 pages.

GOD IS NOT A GENTLEMAN AND I AM THAT ONE
Ecstatic Talks on Conventional Foolishness versus the Crazy Wisdom of
God-Realization
$12.95 paper, 120 pages.

PERIODICALS

THE LAUGHING MAN magazine
The Alternative to Scientific Materialism and Religious Provincialism
2 issues, $12.95

CRAZY WISDOM magazine
The Journal of The Free Daist Communion
(Available only to formal friends, students, and practitioners of the Way of
the Heart) 6 issues, $42.00

CASSETTE TAPES

The ecstatic speech of Heart-Master Da, recorded in gatherings with practitioners during the sixteen years of His Teaching Work, document in part the extraordinary Spiritual Process whereby the True Heart-Master Revealed the Wisdom-Teaching of the Way of the Heart. ($9.95 each):

UNDERSTANDING

THE GOSPEL OF THE SIDDHAS

DEATH IS NOT YOUR CONCERN / THE RITUAL OF SORROW

CHILDREN MUST BE LIBERATED

THE ULTIMATE MUDRA / YOU CAN'T GET THERE FROM HERE

THE ASANA OF SCIENCE

THE BRIDGE TO GOD

KEEP ATTENTION IN THE SACRIFICE

THE FOUNDATION AND THE SOURCE

THE BODILY LOCATION OF HAPPINESS

THE YOGA OF CONSIDERATION AND THE WAY THAT I TEACH

THE COSMIC MANDALA

PURIFY YOURSELF WITH HAPPINESS

THE PRESUMPTION OF BEING

TRANSFORMING SEX AND EVERYTHING / THE ADDICTION AFFLICTION

THE TRANSCENDENCE OF FAMILIARITY

WHAT IS THE CONSCIOUS PROCESS?

A BIRTHDAY MESSAGE FROM JESUS AND ME

FREEDOM IS IN THE EXISTENCE PLACE

THE ULTIMATE WISDOM OF THE PERFECT PRACTICE

FEELING WITHOUT LIMITATION

THE SECRET OF SUDDENNESS

THE KNOWLEDGE OF LIGHT

GOD IS NOT IN CHARGE

USE YOUR ADVANTAGE

CRAZY DA MUST SING, INCLINED TO HIS WEAKER SIDE
*Da Free John [Heart-Master Da] reads His Confessional Poems of
Liberation and Love*

OF THIS I AM PERFECTLY CERTAIN
Ecstatic Readings by Da Free John [Heart-Master Da]
I AM THE HEART OF MAN
A Recitation by Heart-Master Da Free John [Heart-Master Da]

VIDEOTAPES

THE BODILY LOCATION OF HAPPINESS
$59.00, 56 minutes, VHS format

EGO DEATH AND THE CHAOS OF EXPERIENCE
$59.00, 60 minutes, VHS format

THE FIRE MUST HAVE ITS WAY
$59.00, 57 minutes, VHS format

THE TRUTH OF OUR EXISTENCE IS LOVE
$59.00, 60 minutes, VHS format.

Available at local bookstores and by mail from

THE DAWN HORSE BOOK DEPOT
P. O. Box 15260
Seattle, WA 98115 U.S.A.

In the U.S.A. please add $1.50 for the first book or tape and $ .50 for each
additional book or tape. Washington residents add 8% sales tax.

Outside the U.S.A. please add $2.50 for the first book or tape and $ .60 for
each additional book or tape.

Please send for our catalogue of books, audiotapes, videotapes, and
traditional Spiritual literature.

INDEX

AN INVITATION

I f you feel moved to consider Heart-Master Da's Wisdom-Teaching further or to respond to His message of Happiness in any way, we of The Free Daist Communion open our doors and our hearts to assist you.

The Regional Centers of our Communion provide a variety of introductory presentations, programs, and courses to accommodate many levels of interest. At every Regional Center, members of The Free Daist Eleutherian Mission are available to serve your growing understanding and involvement. The Free Daist Eleutherian Mission is the body of practitioners who provide the principal inspirational voice for communication of the Way of the Heart, both in the culture of practitioners and in the public.

For those who do not live near a Regional Center, there are study groups in cities throughout the world.

Additionally, the Regional Centers offer correspondence courses to assist your study of the Wisdom-Teaching of Heart-Master Da in your own home.

For those who wish further involvement, the Lay Member Program will accommodate your interest through guided courses of study, instructive and sacred occasions at our Regional Centers and Sanctuaries around the world, and personal association with practitioners.

Over thirty volumes of the Teaching-Revelation of Heart-Master Da are available. Please write to the address below for a free catalogue of His books, recorded audiotapes and videotapes, and selected traditional and contemporary Spiritual literature. Or, ask us for a free issue of *The Laughing Man* magazine.

If you would like more information about The Free Daist Communion or active forms of patronage and support, or if you would like to become a participating lay member, or if you would like to begin to practice the Way of the Heart, please write to this address:

The Laughing Man Institute
P.O. Box 12775
San Rafael, CA 94913-2775 U.S.A.

Or write or call any of the Regional Centers listed on pp. 137-39 of this book.